For Anna

To Anna, my wife, a special mention for her warmth and encouragement.
There would be no book without her constant support.
Special thanks to Jane Darroch Riley for her design and illustrations and many suggestions that have improved this book.
Thanks to Publio Delgado fro his comments on Chapter VI.
Thanks to Adam Tait for his recording,careful, initial proofreading and advice on Logic. This book would not be what it is without his input.
Thanks to Dror Frangi, Certified Apple Professional, for his deep knowledge of Logic and his advice.
Thanks to Jonathan Stapleton for his careful, final proofreading and editorial comment.
Many thanks to the Emagic and Apple Computer Companies for their assistance during this project.
Logic is a product of the Apple Computer Corporation.

printed in England by Cromwell Press.
© Sheldon Sper 2006
ISBN 978-84-611124-3-1

The author has asserted his right under the Copyright, Designs and Patents Act, 1988, to be identified as the author of this work..

Logic by Arrangement

A quick entry into the
Logic Program through arranging

Present your music in a professional way on CD

Sheldon Sper

Contents:

This book is...

This is the book that I wish I had when first starting to work with the Logic program. The manual was numbing. There was so much material. What was important? What wasn't? What was just an interesting detail that would make life easier but wasn't really crucial. How would I know the difference?

I wanted an intro to the program that would give me the broad strokes yet was not condescending. That would allow me to begin working, even if at a lower level at first. I had learned many computer programs well enough to produce results, without being a power user of that program but, after all, in word processing one does not have to know how to do footnotes or graphics in order to write a good looking letter.

I was writing a show at the time. I wanted to jump right in and learn the program through writing lead sheets, lyrics and arrangements. Later on I wanted to produce reasonable audio demonstration copies of the arrangement and a CD. I longed for a book that would enable me to do simple exercises in arranging and that would lead me step by step to higher levels. And as my arrangements became more complicated I would at the same time learn more of the program which allowed me to create them.

Unfortunately I could not find such a book. Not taking easily to technology, I learned the hard way and it took me several years. The frustration that I suffered and the hours, months and days that I spent in learning could fill another book. The goal of this book is to save you that pain. To make it easier for you to get into Logic quickly by doing everyday tasks in writing and later arranging.

This book is not ...

The biggest difficulty in creating this book was what NOT to write. I had to constantly remind myself that I was writing a guidebook and not a manual. I wanted this book to provide for a person to get started working. And to provide a feel for the program, so that after a time a reader could navigate on his or her own.

Some techniques of arranging are presented and the reader will learn them through practice. This book does not propose to be a textbook of arranging. A systematic presentation of the instruments and all of their uses is not intended; traditional arranging books will do that for you. The purpose of this book is to teach the Logic program and show the quickest and easiest way to realize

normal arranging techniques within Logic. o
Of course I had to discuss harmony, chord types, voicings, tessituras, and the meat of arranging. But I present what every beginner needs to start working. It is not a course in arranging, but it is a good start. This book can be used by a beginner completely new to the program or by an intermediate user interested in making a recording of his work. I would advise the user to follow along and actually do all of the exercises in the book. Even if my style of music is not your bag, the tips and learning that go with the exercises will help you in your other work with the program.

This is not intended as a replacement for the manual. Logic is a very rich program. I explain two levels of recording but the other awesome audio possibilities of the program are barely touched on. After working through a chapter, it is a good idea to check the topics out in the manual for further detailed discussion. Armed with an overview and examples from this book, you will find that the topics suddenly make sense.

Finally, we go through making a simple but presentable audio CD so that you can present your music to others. And to produce good parts for your musicians.

This book will, I hope, become your companion through the beginning stages of a fascinating experience. Best wishes for a good journey!

Sheldon Sper

Chapter I: Versions and Platforms

Version Differences

Since its purchase by Apple Computer in 2002, Logic has undergone a basic marketing change. Before then it served both the PC and the Mac platforms. It also served several price ranges. There were many versions based on cost, which enabled features and capabilities for each version. Development for the PC platform ceased at version 5.5.1. which is, however, still supported. Users were encouraged to cross over to the Mac.

In addition to these versions there was always a junior version. Today the light version is called 'Logic Express'. All of the techniques presented here can be accomplished in various ways in any version of Logic at any price. This includes Logic Pro 7 and Logic Express 7. You might not have the availability of nudge commands to move notes a semitone at a time but you can do the same thing with the arrow key. It is less convenient but it works. You will know when you want to upgrade; you will incur more expense, but gain greater convenience.

There is a 'Logic way' of doing things that has been preserved in all of the versions. Our concerns in this book deal with the way things are done, so much so that the graphic changes made from version to version do not affect us. Where a difference is significant from version to version, as in the 'find' command of versions 6 and 7, it will be specifically explained.

All of the illustrations are from the latest version: Logic 7.

Selecting a tool, Mac

This book assumes you are using the traditional one button mouse, the one that came with your Mac. You select a tool by clicking on it. When you click on another tool it will replaced by the new tool. To use a tool, click on the tool, then click on the item called for. To keep two tools loaded, build in a second click. Click on something and at the same time press the command key. I refer to this as 'command clicking.' Keep the pointer tool as your normal click tool. Load the pencil by command clicking on it. Then, later, to use the pencil, do the same - Command and click. Then your command click will be a pencil-click. This goes for loading any of the tools. The tool or tools will stay loaded until you decide to change tools. I keep the pencil loaded as my second tool.

I recommend a multi-click mouse with a scroll wheel. Several companies manufacture these, both normal and wireless. Your work will go much faster if you use one. For example, you will not need a two handed action to place notes or do the other functions that require a pencil; also moving back and forth between the beginning and end of your arrangement by depressing Command and scrolling the wheel beats using the scroll bars by far. I set up a multi-button mouse as follows: left button - pointer, right button - pencil, additional side button #1 - move the Song Position Line (SPL) forward one bar, additional side button #2 - move the SPL backwards one bar, scroll - scroll. Although I recommend a two button mouse, all of the instructions in this book are for the one button Mac mouse.

On the subject of equipment, I will assume that you have a MIDI piano keyboard that has a few sounds and a sampler or sound module. In the event that you wish to work with virtual instruments, you have the sounds that came with the EXS24. You will want a musical keyboard to 'play in' a part, one way of entering note data.

Selecting a tool, PC

You have a left and a right mouse button. If you place the cursor over a tool and then click, the mouse button that you clicked with will load that tool. For example, if you place the cursor over the pencil and click the right button, every time you click the right button it will be the pencil tool. A handy setting is left button pointer and right button pencil. You can call up the tools as you need them by making Key Commands for them (you learn how to make Key Commands). The tool or tools will stay loaded until you decide to change them. Normally you would keep the pointer tool loaded as the left button.

Other PC – Mac differences

The screens will appear to be slightly different, but they function identically. The Command Keys will be different because the Mac has an additional key which can be used alone or in combination with a key. I create keys using the Mac system but if you are using a PC, replace Command on the Mac by Control on the PC. There will only be problems if there is already a command using both keys. In that case look to any other combination of modifier key (Ctl, Alt or Sh) plus any on the PC that are free. On the PC do not use the arrow keys in combination with Ctl or Alt; there is some hard wiring that will get you mixed up in the menu system. Instead, form a cross with normal keys and with Ctl and Alt for quick correction and manipulation of notes, e.g.

Of course this will depend on the version and language of the keyboard that you are using.

For the sake of uniformity we will use the American English keyboard (at least for our Logic sessions).

Chapter II:
An Overview of Logic

Logic is one of the best multi- function music programs. It enables musicians to hone their skills, make demos, lead sheets, scores and parts, and to record their work. In addition there are commercial uses, such as recordings, musical theater, films and jingles. The program is also used by professional recording studios to produce CDs for mastering.

The program is vast and comprehensive. Few people know all of its intricacies. As with other powerful programs, most users employ only a fraction of its capabilities. One can work for years as a songwriter and only make lead sheets and simple demos without knowing or requiring the advanced audio functions of Logic (mixing, adding effects, tuning up the audio). In the same vein, a person can be a recording genius without knowing much notation. The same applies to other areas of music.

As with most software, once a degree of familiarity is acquired in a program, the user continues on a need-to-know basis. A word of advice to the user: be content to learn enough to do the task at hand. Be patient! You will build up an ever increasing set of skills. Logic provides more than one way to accomplish a task. It won't be long before you can see the most efficient way. Building on this base you will learn to acquire ever increasing knowledge of the program.

This book is intended to enable the beginner to use Logic quickly, while continuing his/her musical work. Along the way to becoming proficient in Logic, one will pick up a lot of arranging know-how and technique. For the uninitiated we will begin with a discussion of the basic concepts. More advanced users can go directly to the next chapter.

The Basic Concepts

The program facilitates three major tasks: writing, editing and recording. In other words: MIDI sequencing/notation, editing and audio. A musician who records a melody on a keyboard and then plays it back is using the MIDI sequencing function. A score is automatically produced which can be printed out. A further accompaniment can be played in, or other MIDI voices can be added and individual parts printed. Other virtual instruments can also be recorded live and added to the mix. Finally, mistakes can be edited and overdubbed. Reverb, panorama and other effects can be added to your MIDI parts (if your sound module, synthesizer or sampler can play them). Finally, audio files can be created which can be further altered (the audio files will use effects like reverb and pan in Logic). This uses all three functions.

You may be interested in using only one aspect of the program. An instrumentalist may only want to record a piano, bass and drum accompaniment. A songwriter may just be interested in lead sheets for piano and voice. An arranger may just want to print parts and scores. However, if any one of these people has to present their music, the program will enable them to make a good demo CD. We will examine each of these functions.

Basic Strategies of the Program

Screens

Logic organizes all of these tasks by means of screensets, each of which does a particular job. You set up the type of musical group you want for your music by selecting its instruments (or just voice and piano for a lead sheet). You make a list of instruments on your master screen called the Environment Screen, assign each instrument to a playback location (channel) and indicate a few characteristics that you want for each instrument, such as how loud it plays, its location on your synthesizer or sound module, and the clef and octave in which it is written. You transfer this information to the Arrange Screen where each instrument has its own track. All the instruments appear together on the Environment Screen. The Environment Screen (there are several sub-screens) shows a graphic representation of all of your equipment.

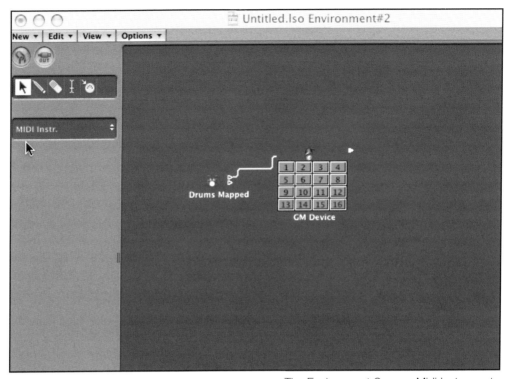

The Environment Screen>Midi Instruments

Open this screen by clicking on >Window >Environment and select the words 'MIDI Instr.' in the selector box at the left of the screen. If they are not there, click and drag until they appear.

As you record a tune by playing your instrument, a score is produced that you may see and edit on a special Score Screen. Or you may just write notes onto staves on that screen with your mouse and then play them back. You may sequence a recording in the Arrange Screen by playing your synthesizer after pressing the record button.

Other screens show you the notes you have played or written in different forms and allow you to modify them. You may change or correct the pitch or duration of the note or modify its volume.

The Environment Screen>A Mixer

Of course you cannot record unless you have a mixer to control volume and other data basic to recording. If you are using Logic's virtual instruments you do this using an audio mixer, also found in the Environment.

Multiple Screens

Later in this chapter we will create composite or multiple screens. They combine screens and simplify your use of the program. Multiple screensets give a multifaceted view of Logic. They streamline the process by allowing you to work without having to continually open the same screens.

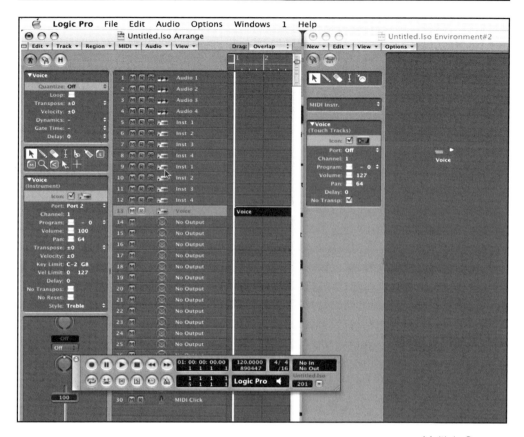

Multiple Screens

You can create a split combination screen of Arrange and the Environment to help assign your instruments; or combine the Score Screen with a mixing table to follow the score as you adjust the dynamics or tempi.

Everything that happens in the program happens on every screen at the same time, even on those screens that you do not see. So when you open a screen in an arrangement for the first time, you will know that the data are already there waiting for you.

You can create multiples of three or more screens if your monitor is large enough. The truly zealous can also work with more than one monitor but we will not discuss that here. One medium screen can comfortably support

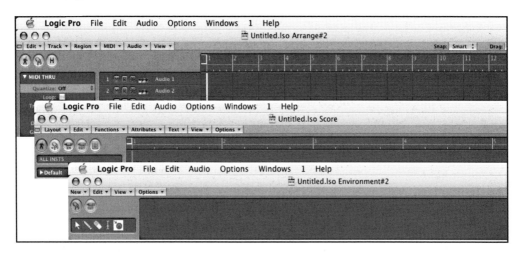

Menus

Menus are located at the top of each screen. Each menu offers multiple choices, some of them leading to further menus, others directly to single choice items. The menus are constructed so that the choices pertaining to score are mostly on the Score Screen, the choices devoted to audio are on the Audio Screen, etc. You will soon become familiar with the choices. We show menu choices by using the symbol >.

Key Commands

Finally, there is a third system that mediates between the screens and the menus. A press of a single key, or of a key in combination with [alt ⌥], [⇧], [ctrl], [⌘], has the same effect as making a menu choice or selecting something with the mouse. [PC users: you must make adjustments for the lack of a Command key] This shortcut method allows you to work very quickly when you know which menu choices you want or if the commands are repetitive. For example, a key command to move the Song Position Line or SPL is much easier to manage than moving the SPL with the mouse. You can do it both ways; it is a feature of Logic that the same task can be done in more than one way. Not only do the Key Commands substitute for the Menu commands, in addition there are some functions that can be accessed only by key commands.

Although the platform for the present program, Logic Pro 7, is Mac, there are still many existing versions of Logic written for PC. Both perform the same functions as far as we are concerned. Since the Mac has three modifier keys and the PC only two, the work is allocated differently to each. In this book Mac commands are given, since PC users can see the equivalent key commands printed in the menus. PC users open the Key Command Screen with ctrl + K ; Mac users with alt + K .

Let's examine the various screens to learn about their functions and possibilities.

Arrange Screen

Press [⌘] + [↑] to open the Arrange Screen. You have just used a Key Command.
In Logic the screens are pre-programmed. You can see these assignments
by opening Key Commands ([alt] + [K]) and scrolling to the 'Global Commands'
section. You can also open the Arrange Screen by selecting it using Windows
>Arrange . Later we will add our own screen sets. You may wish to enlarge
the screen. Either use the sliders at the right top or left bottom of the Arrange
Screen (Logic 7) or click on the large side of the telescope, located at the top
right of the screen (previous versions of Logic). You can also use [ctrl] + [↑] or
[↓] and [ctrl] + [→] or [←] to enlarge or diminish the contents of the screens.

To widen one track, you can also use > View >Autotrack Zoom of the Arrange
Screen. Alternatively, you can pull the bottom of the track to the left of its
name downwards. As previously mentioned, the ability to achieve the same
result in many ways is a feature of Logic.

The Arrange Screen is central to the program. It contains the sequences (or
objects) of the arrangement, MIDI or audio. This screen shows all of the work
you have done from the beginning of the arrangement to the end. It is the only
screen that unites both types of data.

For large arrangements, sequences can be identified by labeling. For labeling
sequences, the text tool , ▌ , is used.

The Environment Screen

EnvironmentScreen

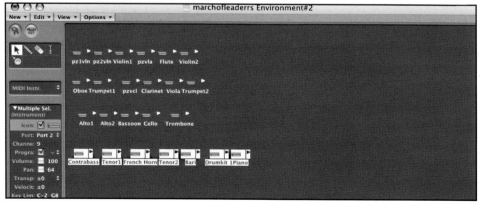

Press ⌘+8 to open the Environment Screen. The Environment displays your hardware and helps you to manage it. The channel and port assignments of your instruments are displayed. Other devices are also available to manipulate the path of the stream of MIDI data

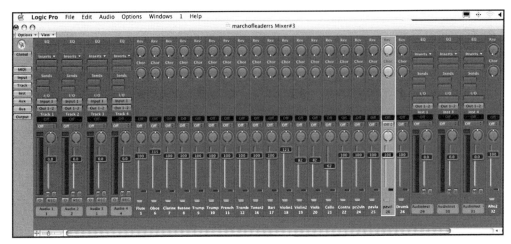

Mixers

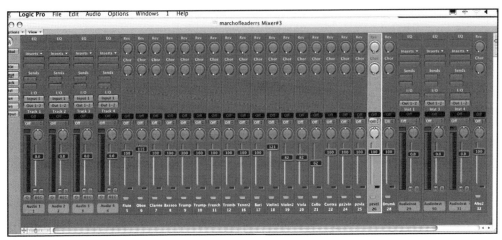

Mixers

Mixers

There are two mixers provided with Logic, a Track Mixer and an Audio Mixer. The Track Mixer shows the mixable equipment on the tracks of the Arrange Screen (the MIDI instruments, the virtual instruments, the audio channels you have put there for your arrangement). The Audio Mixer shows all the audio equipment in the environment, both used and available to be used, that is present in the program. The difference is not important at this moment, because you can always create equipment like Audio Channels or virtual instrument mixer strips when you need them, if your program does not already have them. The Audio Mixer is called up by >Audio >Audio Mixer. Calling up the Environment Screen first also gets you, via the selection rectangle, to the Audio Mixer. The menu command >Windows >Track Mixer calls up the Track Mixer, as does ⌘+2 .

In addition to these mixers, advanced users can create their own. An example follows. Either mixer can be used for recording. Remember, the Track Mixer is a representation of tracks on the Arrange screen. With 'global' checked, you see all the instruments available in the Environment: virtual, audio and MIDI.

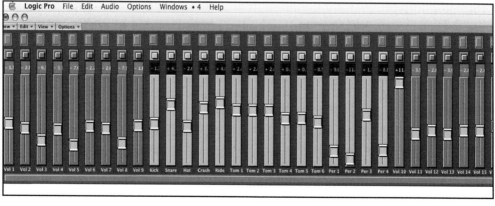

Hand-built Mixer

The Score Screen

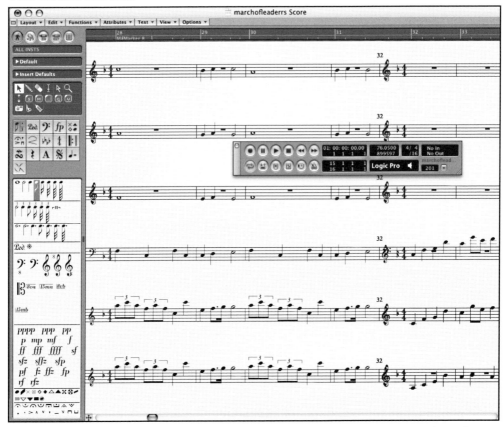

Score Screen

Press ⌘+#3 to open the Score Screen.

The Score Screen shows the sequenced notes in notation form. Also you can add notes here by inputting them on your synthesizer (step input), writing them in with the mouse, or creating them from the virtual keyboard in >Windows >Step Input Keyboard. You can also 'play them in' here or in the Arrange Screen. The Score Screen is also one of the major screens that you use to modify the notes. A sequence can be played on any screen by selecting the 'play' button on the transport. The sequence is played from the Song Position Line (SPL) as mentioned previously. The space bar can also be used for 'play' or we can assign a key command to it later.

The Matrix Screen

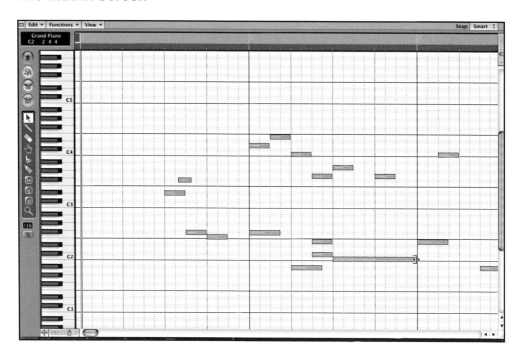

Press ⌘+6 to open the Matrix Screen.

The Matrix Screen represents your notes in piano-roll style. Initially the Matrix Screen displays a single instrument part, but if you double-click on the background of the screen, all of the parts will be displayed. Very often it is easier to work with single parts. Your mistakes are best spotted on the Matrix screen. For example one can see if a note is out of position or too long. Fortunately, these are easy to correct. Clicking on the bottom right of the note will produce the bracket with which you can shorten or lengthen the note by dragging as you can see in the illustration above. Non Logic 7 users: you get a pointing finger instead. Alternatively you can choose the pointing finger tool yourself from among the tools, with which you can easily elongate the notes. If you click anywhere else on the note you produce a clenched hand icon , which allows you to move the note in its entirety. These actions affect a note's staff position and length. You can achieve a fine movement of the finger, hand or any pointing device by holding down alt when editing, and a finer movement yet using ctrl + alt .

2 Parts, 2 Matrix Screens

The Matrix Screen will open the staff that has been previously selected. If you want to see all of the parts, double-click on the screen background. If you want to see only two parts, open Matrix twice (in single part form) by selecting one staff and opening the Matrix Screen then selecting the other staff and opening the screen again. Make sure the link icon in the matrix edit is unlit.

If you are recording the notes from the Arrange Screen (by playing), there may be some overlap between notes. If two instruments play the same notes, one note is placed on top of the other. To see and correct the lengths and timing of all of the notes you may temporarily move a note or two out of the way, correct the note that is left, then move another note on top of it, correct that note, and repeat the process if necessary.

The Event List

Use >Window to open the Event List Screen.

You also have a screen which lists each MIDI event. This allows you to make or add changes in another way. This screen tells the user exactly when something has

Event List Screen

Position				Status	Cha	Num	Val	Length/Info	
1	3	1	1	Note	1	D#3	64	. . 1	232
1	3	2	81	Note	1	F#3	64	. . 1	72
1	3	3	1	Note	1	F#2	64	. . 1	232
1	4	1	1	Note	1	F2	64	. . 1	232
2	1	1	1	Note	1	F#2	64	. . 2	232
2	1	1	1	Note	1	D4	64	. . 1	232
2	1	3	1	Note	1	E4	64	. . 1	232
2	2	1	1	Note	1	A#1	64	. . 2	232
2	2	1	1	Note	1	C4	64	. . 1	232
2	2	3	1	Note	1	C#2	64	. . 1	232

occurred, on which channel and to which degree. A MIDI event can be a note, along with its duration, location and pitch. It can also be a program change, pitchbend, aftertouch, modulation or myriad other controller data. The location and timing of each event is noted by measure and part of the measure (example, the 3rd beat of measure 2). You can create an event and insert it anywhere in the score. It is a precise way to enter information into the program.

The Transform Screen

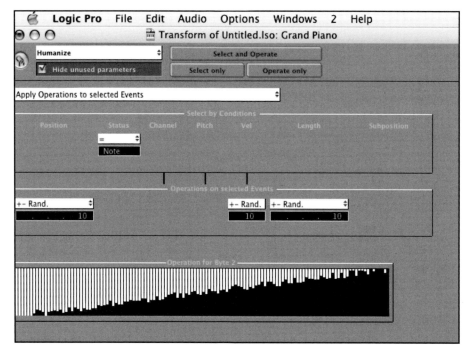

The Transform Screens

Press ⌘+s/4 to open the Transform Screen.

The Transform Screen changes streams of MIDI data, such as notes, according to the instructions you give it. You can transform sequences, single parts or whole songs in many ways. We will focus on this screen's ability to 'humanize' a part. Two live musicians playing together sound alive and vibrant. In contrast, if you were to copy a mouse-made flute part to a clarinet part and then play them together they would sound a little disappointing, somewhat mechanical. When we examine the differences between the human and the MIDI performances we understand why. Because the flute and clarinet part are machine made and perfect, they always play the note on time and for its full duration. The little inconsistencies and hesitations, the shadings of loud and soft, are not there. Hence they sound mechanical.

On the other hand, because they are humans and not machines, our musicians try to play identically, but each one phrases differently, holds the notes longer or shorter than the other, breathes differently. This difference is very human and adds a dimension that gives the playing warmth and life . One of the many functions of this screen is to differentiate the parts in this 'human' way. This is one of many ways of giving extra life to your recording.

The Hyperedit Screen

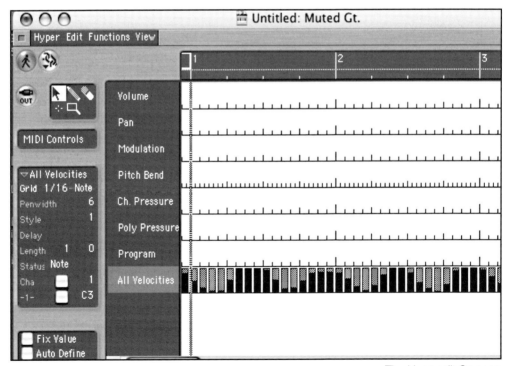

The Hyperedit Screens

Press ⌘+% to open the Hyperedit Screen.
This screen makes changes in the course of the song that affect the

performances on any channel in respect to volume, velocity or any other effect that you have enabled through the MIDI controllers. You can change the effects, for example, in velocity and volume. 'Velocity' is the 'gusto' with which you play the instrument (how hard you strum the guitar, how hard you blow the trumpet); 'volume' is the sheer loudness of the instrument (how high your amplifier is turned up).

You can pencil in velocity or volume changes throughout the course of the performance. First you choose the channel whose performance you want to affect. Then you pencil in the degree of velocity you desire. You will get the hang of this with a little practice. The screen on the left illustrates the undulating velocity of an instrument over the course of two bars of a song.

Hyperdraw

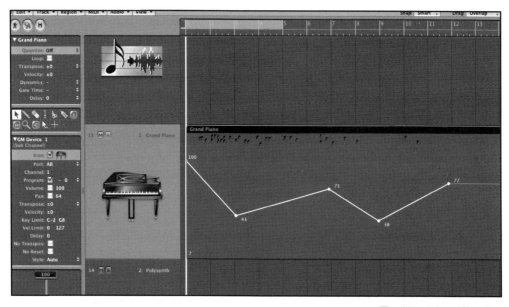

The Hyperdraw Screens

You open Hyperdraw through the >View >Hyperdraw menu on the Arrange Screen, the Score Screen and the Matrix Screen. This makes sense because you can follow (and affect) the course of an entire song easily on these screens.

This function usually operates on individual channels. This is one way that you can give more prominence to a soloist or get a blended section sound.

The blue Hyperdraw Window appears below the selected track it is attached to. The track has to be wide, to display Hyperdraw. You know how to widen an individual track: all of the tracks can be simultaneously altered in size by using the methods previously mentioned, such as the slider. Alternatively, one could use the function >View >Auto Track Zoom of the Arrange Screen. You can create nodes, which are points of change in volume, panning, instrument, pitch bend, and other functions–depending on which of these functions is chosen–by clicking the mouse. In a later chapter we will see real examples of Hyperdraw when we are preparing our work for recording.

The control of Hyperdraw and Hyperedit are identical in many ways. Again, this is just another example of Logic doing the same thing in several different ways. Choose the method that best fits the situation.

Multiple screens

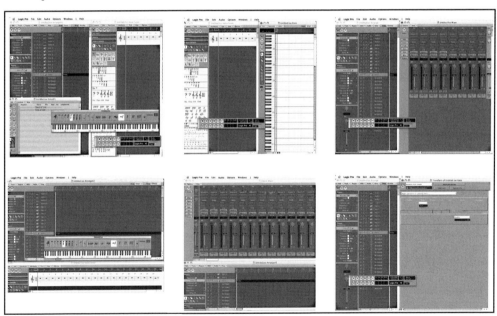

Multiple Screens

To complete this section on screens, it is worth mentioning again that you will often work going back and forth between two or three screens. Multiple screens give a multifaceted view of Logic. It keeps you from having to continually open the same screens. You can monitor twice as much information if you have two screens in front of you. If you have a medium sized monitor you can create multiple screens. Both screens remain visible if they are side by side and do not overlap. Overlapping causes the top screen to change places with the screen directly below it. This can be used now as long as you remain aware of which screen is on the bottom. If you are constantly going back and forth between screens, you can make them alternate by overlapping them or keeping them immobile.

Alternatively, you could multiply your screens by using more than one monitor. There are different configurations of graphic cards and monitor types that you could use. A lot of professionals use two or three screens.

The Transport Bar and SPL

The SPL

Most of your screens have a work window to the right which takes up most of the screen and a parameter box or two on the left hand side. Along the top and side of the work window is a ruler which shows the measures and a vertical line which marks your location in the song. This line is called the Song Position Line or SPL. The SPL can be found on the Arrange, Score, Matrix and Hyper Edit Screens. By illuminating the 'running man' 🏃 tracking butto in these screens (also on the top left) you will ensure that the current SPL is always visible, whether during recording or play-back.

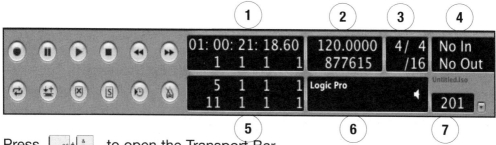

Press ⌘+& to open the Transport Bar.

The final screen to mention is the Transport Bar. It is called a floating screen because it appears on top of existing screens and does not disappear when you go from screen to screen. It is used partly for information and partly for controlling the playback and rewind of your sequence, your tempo and location.

The first line of control buttons from left to right are: record, pause, play, stop and rewind for either direction. The second line of control buttons are: cycle mode, drop in, replace, solo, sync, and metronome. Cycle mode allows you to play or record between certain measures. These measures are shown in the window to the right. In our illustration the song is set to cycle between measures 5 and 11. The window above shows you where the SPL is in both SMPTE time, and in bars and beats.

'Drop-in' is a technique used in recording for correction. It is useful when you have screwed up one section of an otherwise brilliant solo. 'Replace' is a sophisticated paste function that allows you to overwrite an old sequence with the data from your current cycle mode. 'Solo' is a useful feature that isolates the selected music from the whole. When a whole orchestra is playing, it helps one to distinguish individual instruments. 'Sync' means time coordination to an external device, such as a multi-track tape, or the clock of an external CD. Finally, the metronome button leads to the settings which enable you to choose which instrument will act as the time marker. In addition, you can choose the divisions of the beat that you want marked, and which instrument shall mark it and how loud each beat is. Your other option deals with recording settings, such as the number of lead-in bars and other work preferences.

There are six small windows on the right side of the Transport Bar:

The first window, labeled 1, shows the location of the SPL in two formats: SMPTE time (hours:min:sec:frames), and bars and beats.

Window 2 sets your tempo on the top line. The bottom line, if double-clicked on, will allow you to refresh (reconfigure) the memory in the memory buffer.

Window 3 configures the time signature. The fraction on the bottom, called the division setting, indicates which grid value you are using for adjustments. If this value is set to 1/16 you move or lengthen the note value by a sixteenth note; if the division is set to 2 you affect the note by a half note value, etc.

Time is set up on a grid, the finest division of a note being 1/192 of a measure. We cannot play that accurately, but when working in the matrix I prefer to set the grid up very high .

Window 4 indicates the flow of MIDI data in or out of the program. It is good for diagnostics. If you see a MIDI flow out but hear nothing, you should start checking the audio signal. If you hear nothing and see no MIDI action you should start by checking your MIDI hookup.

Window 5 shows the location in bars of the cycle mode (locators).

Window 6, with the Emagic name display, shows the location of the drop bars when recording with that option (when cycle mode is on).

Window 7 shows the allowable length of the song in bars. You can make your arrangement longer, if necessary, by changing this number.

The button at the far right gives you menu choices which allow you to custom configure your Transport Bar. You may want to alter its size. One useful custom feature is the position slider at the bottom of the Transport Bar which allows you to move the SPL to an approximate location.

In earlier versions than Logic 7, there were four vertical buttons in the center. The top button toggled up the marker list. The second button moved the SPL to the nearest rounded bar, if pressed again, to the left locator and, if pressed a third time, to the beginning of the song. The third and fourth buttons moved the SPL to the left and right locators, respectively.

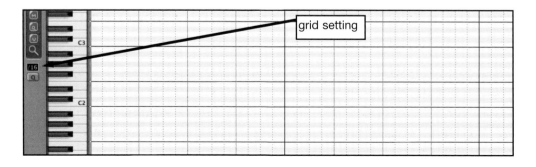

grid setting

Chapter III: First Steps - A Lead Sheet

Here we are, in front of the computer, with a blank screen in front of us and a song in our hearts ready to be entered in note form with piano or guitar accompaniment and a particular singer in mind. You can't wait to get it printed. It is a song, with lyrics, written for your performer. We are going to copy my song 'Again'.

'Again', in appendix I,A is a song I wrote which is in leadsheet form. It has chords for a singer and accompanist: usually a piano or guitar. Photocopy it or remove it from the book for easy copying to Logic.

In copying this leadsheet I will show you how I set up both MIDI and virtual instruments. Along the way I will show you some alternative methods for copying and inputting notes to the program. We will learn how to create a staff and how to copy from one place to another; and how the copy process is used to create newer sections of our lead sheet. We will learn what we have to know about inputting lyrics and chords, the essentials of the lead sheet. Jazz pianists can play accompaniments just by reading the chord symbols alone and do not require written chords. What you should remember is that I am showing you my preferred way of doing things. The program is rich enough to allow for variation; you will soon do things your own way.

Instrument set-up

You have just booted up a new blank song. The first thing you see is an Arrange Screen with many tracks. There are audio tracks, virtual instrument tracks and other instrument tracks. These instrument tracks are MIDI related for synthesizer voices or voice modules. The audio-instrument tracks are for virtual voices, and the audio tracks for (creating) recording and playing soundwaves. More on audio tracks and audio-instrument tracks later. We will concern ourselves first with MIDI instrument voices.

Arrange Screen

Setting up MIDI instruments

I suggest that you read this section even if you do not use sound modules or synthesizers. Select the menu choice >Windows, then select the Environment Screen.

You are now in the Midi Instruments sub-screen of the Environment Screen. It is one of the sub-screens of the Environment. You can examine the Environment a bit by selecting and dragging on the words in the choice rectangle of the Environment Screen and examining each screen.

Return to the MIDI Instr. sub-screen. You will put in place an icon of an instrument named 'Voice' which will appear on the Arrange and Environment Screens, depicting the chosen instrument. It shows a note and a waveform representing the alto sax singing the melody. If you are not working with a sound module there is information geared towards virtual sounds which you will find in a moment. Read on!

For practice we will create an instrument. Make a new instrument by selecting >New >Instrument from the menu. It will then be highlighted. To simplify for printing, name the instrument 'voice'. Rename the instrument by clicking on the parameter box and typing in a name.

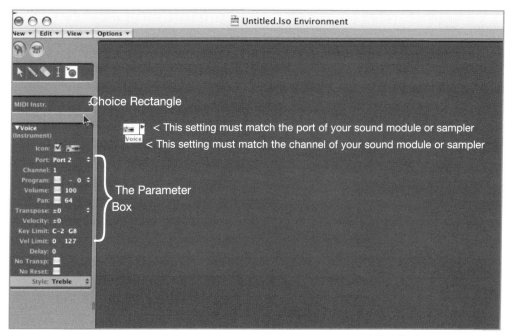

The Environment Screen

Look at the parameter box at the left of the Environment Screen. I have made changes that agree with my instrument set-up. Yours may be different. The channel number in the parameter box at the left is set to '1'. It could be any channel as long as it matches the channel number on your sound module.

Also, if you have a MIDI interface hooked up to several devices, be sure to connect it to the port that your sound device is connected to. For example, if your sound module is connected to port 2 and your sampler is connected to port 3 (of your MIDI interface), make sure your port settings correspond. Even if you have a MIDI interface with only two ports, they must correspond.

Click on the instrument icon in the parameter box and hold the mouse down. You will get a sub-screen of icons that enables you to choose one that best suits the instrument. In this case we have chosen a musical note with soundwave.

At this point, you should also change the clef choice 'auto' at the bottom of the parameter box by clicking and holding it down. You will get a rectangular sub-screen of clef choices.

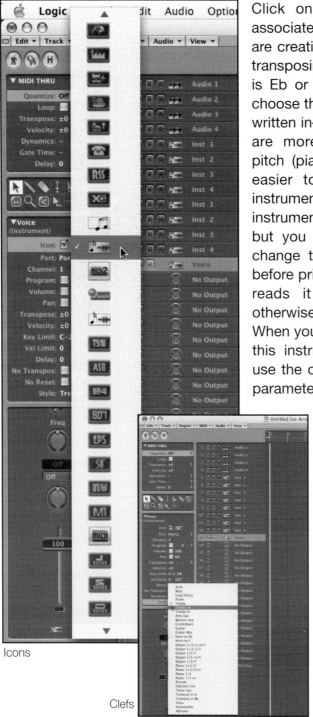

Icons

Clefs

Click on the clef that is usually associated with the instrument you are creating. If you are writing for a transposing instrument where 'doh' is Eb or Bb instead of C, you can choose the clef that the instrument is written in–say, Eb for alto sax. If you are more comfortable in concert pitch (piano pitch), you may find it easier to choose treble for high instruments and bass clef for low instruments for working with now, but you will have to remember to change to the transposed clef just before printing (so that the trumpeter reads it as he normally does), otherwise a musical mess will result. When you make additional staves for this instrument it will automatically use the clef you have chosen in the parameter box.

Change the volume to '60' by clicking on the number in the parameter box and dragging the mouse or by double-clicking on the number and typing a new number in the box that appears. This governs the base volume of playback while you are working. You could start out a combo group with a pre-set of volume, program (voice) and pan parameters.

We will now finish configuring the voice instrument on the Arrange Screen. To do this you must create a multiple screen, placing the Arrange Screen on the left and the Environment Screen on the right. The first step in creating a multiple screen is to open the Arrange Screen and then reduce its size by half using the sizer in the lower right hand corner of the window. Then open the Environment Screen and reduce it in size to match.

Multiple Screens

Be sure to arrange the screens so that they do not overlap. You can do this by hand, in which case you can make the screens unequal in size and place them in custom positions, or you can make them equal and side by side, or horizontal by 'tiling' them. See >Windows >Tile or >Tile Horizontally. You may move the screens by dragging them with the pointer on the name strip at the top of the screen. If the screens overlap, as you go from screen to screen, one screen will disappear behind the other. This constant hide and seek can waste a lot of time and be very tedious. Knowing this, you can move the screens this way to your advantage. If you know that the screen you want to use is hiding behind the present screen that is in front of it, you can just click on it to move it to the forefront.

To create a "Screenset" of a single screen or of multiple screens, first erase all screens. Make your single screen the way you want it or build your desired grouping of screens, calling them up and sizing and moving them. Press ⟦⇧⟧ + a number, if you are saving the screenset to a single digit number. If you wish to save to double digit numbers press ⟦ctrl⟧+⟦⇧⟧ and the number. To recall the saved screenset, use the number or ⟦ctrl⟧ if it is a double-digit number. It is good to use ⟦⇧⟧+⟦L⟧ to keep these screensets 'locked' so that they cannot be changed. This method of saving screens as multi-screens will work on any number of screens up to 99. Making a large array of screensets, some zoomed, some multiple, takes time but ultimately saves time.

Click on the icon of the instrument, (the musical note and waveform, in this case) in the Environment Screen, and pull it to the first available instrument track in the Arrange Screen. The settings and icon are transferred from one screen to the other.

An alternative method

We will make a brief side step here to show you an alternative method of establishing instruments on the Arrange Screen. First you must clear up the material you have created doing the first method. The easiest way is to close without saving and call up a new song. The program opens on a clean, new Arrange Screen. Open the Environment Screen and create and name a new instrument with >New and >Instrument. Choose the text tool and click on 'new instrument' and change the name to 'voice'.

This is remark thas nothing to do with the operation of the program. Some people like to erase all tracks that are not being used from the Arrange and create tracks only when needed. You create a new instrument track with ⟦⇧⟧+⟦↵⟧

You convert it to whichever track you desire using the procedure we are going to show next. Erase all tracks from the Arrange Screen.

You are going to change an instrument track in the Arrange Screen to a track for the voice instrument you have just created in the Environment Screen. Click and hold on the instrument name. You get a rectangular sub-screen. One of its choices is MIDI instruments. Still holding down the mouse, drag the pointer over to 'voice' and release. This establishes the instrument and the track is now called 'voice' and has the parameters that you set in the Environment Screen.

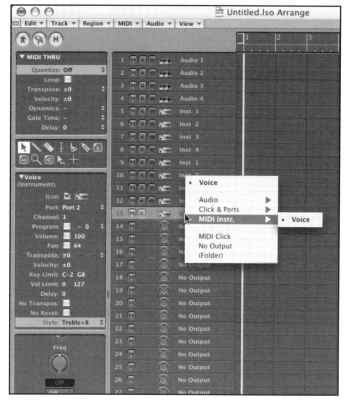

You have previously erased all of the tracks on the Arrange Screen. You can create them by menu choice in this screen under >Track >Create Track or by keyboard command ⇧+↵ For an instrument track, choose a MIDI instrument (already introduced in the environment); for an audio channel choose 'audio' at this point, etc.

Of the two methods, the first procedure–the multiple screen and dragging the icon–was easier, wasn't it? You can use either method.

For practice, go back to the Environment Screen and create three other instruments. Designate a different channel, name and icon for each one.

Open the Arrange Screen and establish these instruments on separate tracks by making a split screen and click-dragging their respective icons from the Environment or by the second method: clicking and holding on their respective icons. You do not have to erase since you are going to initialize the program before setting up the virtual instruments.

Now we return from our diversion to set up another kind of instrument.

Setting up Virtual Instruments

Start with a clean slate. Initialize the program and start with a new song. Virtual Instruments have been around for years and have become a cornerstone of modern production. It is possible (and widely done) to make a recording using nothing but a virtual orchestra. If you do not have Virtual Instruments or only the few supplied with the program, that should not hinder you from using the rest of this book. Those of you who have the small set of samples supplied by Apple can use them here.

Virtual Instruments

If you are working with the virtual sounds in EXS24 you first locate the EXS24. You select > Audio >Audio Mixer from the menu. Or press ⌘+⑨ which will give you the Track Mixer. Make sure the 'global' rectangle is chosen, if not choose it.

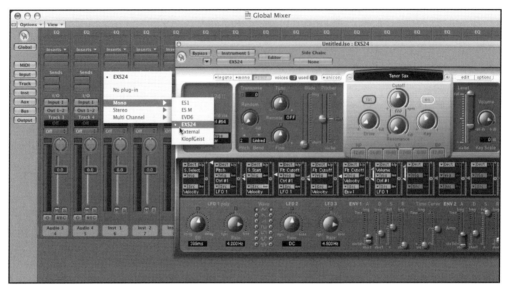

EXS24

Using the scroll bar on the bottom of the mixer screen, go to any audio-instrument channel strip (a good idea is to start all your audio and audio-instrument tracks at track 1 in numbered sequence in the mixer to maintain order), and click on the top input just above outputs 1-2. Choose mono effect >Logic>EXS24.

The Virtual Instrument screen appears. Click and hold on the instrument window until your instruments appear. You have a tenor sax in 'factory' on the CD disk that came with the program. The sample sounds (and all sounds) are put in a 'sample directory' in the program directory. Load the tenor sax.

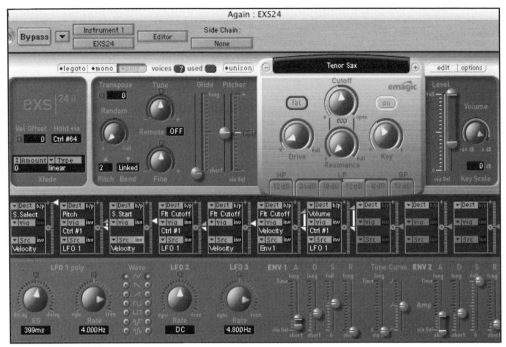

Tenor Sax

Open the Arrange Screen by choosing >Windows >Arrange Screen from the menu. You do not have to get out of the EXS24 screen and the track mixer before doing this. Just press ⌘+1 on the keyboard above the letters. The window will open automatically.

In the track 'audio-instrument 1' the channel is designated as 'Instrument 1' in the parameter box at the left of the screen and the MIDI channel as '1'. Leave those settings alone. Click on the instrument icon in the parameter box and hold the mouse down. As with the MIDI instruments you get a sub-screen of icons that enable you to choose one that best fits the instrument. With the text tool, you may change the instrument track name to whatever you choose. You can choose the note and soundwave icon again and label the track A1 (for Audio-Instrument 1) and 'voice' for printing purposes. I called it Voice on the Arrange and Environment Screens. The icon helps identify the instrument, the label identifies it definitively. Change the clef in 'Style' to the instrument's habitual clef.

For practice, go back to the track mixer and EXS24 sampler and repeat the process by entering two more i n s t r u m e n t s , designating a different name (for the instrument) and icon for each one. Remember to adjust their names and usual clef. This is good practice for when you set up a group of instruments for a combo or big band.

Erase all of these instruments except the sax from the Arrange Screen by selecting the track and then pressing the backspace key. This will not automatically remove the instruments from the Environment Screen, so erase these tracks now. It makes for a clean work space to remove all tracks from the Arrange Page except the track that you are working on. You can create the tracks again when you need them.

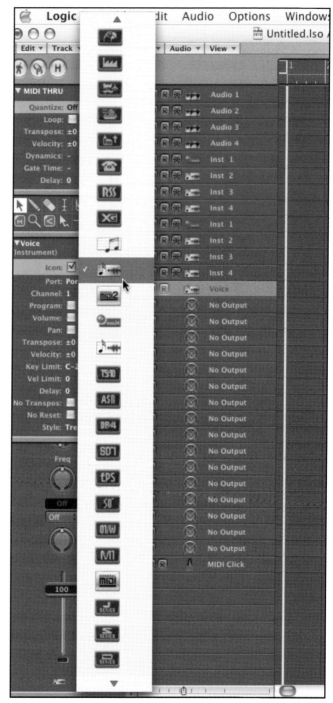

Icons

Group select

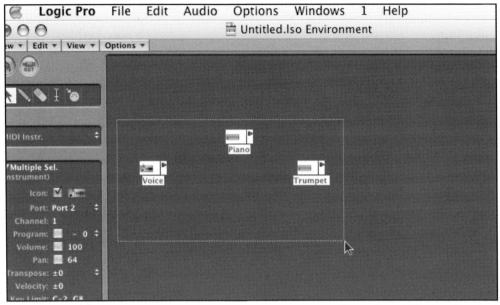

Group Select 'Rubber Banding'

Before we get into the actual copying of the lead sheet we shall take a few interesting and useful digressions into the selecting of several objects, the Instrument Set and Score Styles windows and creating the staff.

Open the, MIDI Instruments sub-screen in the Environment Screen. Create three new MIDI instruments with >New. Group select (also called 'rubber band select') the three instruments. This is achieved by clicking on the background and holding and moving the pointer to cover and include the objects you wish to select. When the objects are covered, release the mouse button. The selected objects are highlighted and ready for whatever operation you have in mind. We will delete the three together rather than deleting them one at a time. Press the backspace to delete. Later on you will be group selecting notes, bars, all sorts of objects in this program.

Another useful feature of group select is in allocating the same instrument parameters, such as name or volume level. With 'new' and 'instrument', create four instruments which you name 'trumpet'. Make the text tool your working tool. Rubberband select all of the trumpet sounds. For the sake of this example change the name of the instrument to 'trump' plus the number '1' in the parameter box; the name will be 'Multiple' because of the multiple selection. Change to the arrow tool and enter '60' under volume. Deselect the three instruments and check each one; the volume setting will be identical. But the name will be 'trump1, trump2, trump3,' and so on. If you had named the instruments 'trumperino' without the number, for the purpose of testing, you would find all the instruments named 'trumperino'. You have set all three instruments by the power of rubberbanding. This tip will come in handy later when you have five saxes and four trombones and in many other situations. Remember it!

Let us get acquainted with a feature integral to Logic, the Song Position Line or SPL. Open the Arrange Screen, call up the Transport Bar using >Windows> Transport. Click on the stop button [◉] . That brings the Song Position Line (SPL) to the beginning of the song. The program is designed so that if a song is playing the first click on stop button will stop it and a further click on it will rewind the SPL to the beginning (unless you are in cycle: then the first click is 'stop'; second is the left locator and third is 'rewind to beginning'.

Two powerful windows, Instrument Set and Score Styles

Choose >Score from the menu choice >Windows. You use >Layout >Instrument Sets or a Key Command to call up this screen. You get to the Score Screen by selecting a staff then 'Style' in the upper parameter box. Let us make two frequently used key commands before going on. Assign ⌘+ctrl+I to Instrument Sets and ⌘+ctrl+S to Score Styles. To do this, open the Key Command Screen with alt+K and type 'set' in the query box at the top right (or the 'Find' box in older versions). The commands containing the word 'set' appear at the lower end of the command screen. Select the command on the screen (it will darken), select the 'learn' option and press the ⌘+ctrl+I keys and release them. You will see the Command, Control and I written next to 'Open Instrument Set Window' on the same line. Select 'Open Score Styles Window' and press ⌘+ctrl+S . Turn off 'learn' and close Key Commands and you are done.

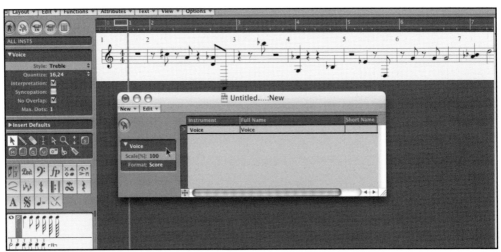

Accessing Instrument Set

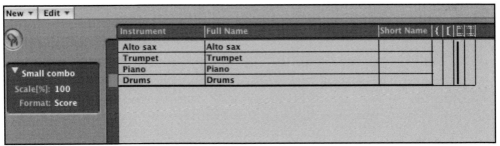

Instrument Set Window

This is only an introduction to Instrument Set, this important window. Here is where you put the instruments that you want to appear on the score sheet and, ultimately, on the paper. You can have many different trumpets playing to contribute to an overall trumpet sound but if you only put the sweet trumpet on the instrument set list, only the sweet trumpet will appear on the screen. The staccato trumpet will play but not be seen unless you list it here. You can avoid duplication of the staves when printing. You can also choose to not show parts, clicking on the 'M' of the instument track or with the'M' key command. The instument set shows the instrument you chose to see. E.g.: you can edit the saxes by making an instrument set, but you can hear the whole orchestra while doing so. You can create and have dozens of different instrument sets. If you erase them before printing, unwanted trumpets will not print out; you find only one trumpet part on the print-out.

This window is also where you can create the list of instruments that you work on at any one time. You do not have to have all of the instruments in front of you while you are working with the saxophones. Temporarily list the instruments you wish to work on in an instrument set, put that instrument set in place and narrow your workplace; you can recall the other instruments at any time to see how your work fits into the whole.

Score Styles is important for printing. You can designate the particular clef and its size, the distance of one line from the next, the degree of slant of the beams, whether the beams are placed above or below the note etc. Changes are made by drag-clicking. Under 'Clef' change 'treble' to 'bass'. The treble clef on the score will change to bass. Other changes are made in the same way.

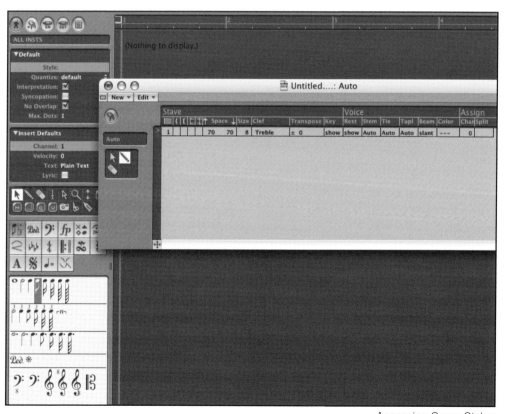

Accessing Score Styles

You want to be sure that all the instruments are set in the appropriate clef for them. Otherwise there would be a terrible cacophony when they play. Pay special attention to the transposing instruments. Change the trumpet from treble (concert) to Bb Trumpet so that the part will be read correctly by trumpeters. Do the same for the saxophone, clarinet and other transposing instruments. An orchestration or arranging book is called for here to understand this, but in Logic you will make the correct transpositions by choosing the correct clef. It makes the correct changes, such as trumpet and clarinet to Bb and Alto and Baritone sax to Eb. You set the correct clef here in Score Styles. It should appear on the top left of the Score Screen with the other instrument characteristics.

Both of these screens are used so frequently that they should be assigned a key commmand–which you have done.

Go back to the Arrange Screen. Erase without saving and call up a new empty song. You now have a copy on paper of the lead sheet we are going to copy and a blank program in front of you.

Creating a Staff

Assign the pencil tool to your one-button mouse or assign it to the right button of your two-button mouse. Then, with the pencil tool, click on bar one, beat one of your instrument track. A little black rectangle appears. If you were to look in Score you would see a staff of one bar. Make sure that the left hand side of the rectangle is set on measure 1. If not, click and drag the little rectangle into place. Select it with the pointer, grab it at the lower right hand corner until you see the bracket (in earlier versions the pointing finger) and, still holding the button down, pull the block to the right to bar 30.

Open the Score Screen. We are now going to enter music in the most elementary way. You should have a staff running across the page from left to right.

Creating a Staff

Using the menu, choose View >Instrument Names to be sure which name has been assigned to the instrument(s) on the screen. This becomes more important when you have many staves and instruments to keep track of. You'll want to make a key command for this function since you will use it frequently.

Open the Key Command Screen. To locate the command you want to change, quickly use the query box in the upper right hand corner and type the first few letters of the command you are searching for.

Instrument Names

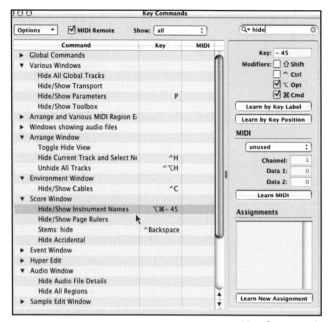

Key Commands

You type 'hide', because you are looking for command: 'Hide/Show Instrument Names' Logic 7 will show you all the commands with 'hide' in them. In Logic 6 and previous, highlight the 'find' box of key commands and highlight and type next to it 'hide' and return.

One of the choices containing the string 'Hide' will be 'Hide/Show Instrument Names'. Assign to it the keys ⌘+alt ⌥+N .

Returning to the Score Screen, use the mouse to make sure the [🎧] icon at the top left of the page is clicked on. This means 'MIDI out', and allows you to hear each note as you enter it.   On the left hand edge of the page you have a selection of icons, one of which relates to the notes. Click on the appropriate one. We are going to enter the first eight bars of the song.

To enter an eighth note, click on the eighth note icon [🎵🎼🎼] move the mouse pointer to the staff where you want to place the note, and then pencil-click. The note should appear on the staff 🎼 . Return to the part box and pencil-click on another note value. Then go back to the staff and pencil-click again. Another note should appear.

If you want to enter an eighth triplet, you must be sure the Quantization setting at the top left of the screen is set to '8-12' or higher. The '8' allows you to display eighth notes and the '8-12' allows for eighth notes and four sets of triplet eighths.   If you are going to enter sixteenth notes, the quantization must be set to at least '16' and for sextuplets, '16-24' . The same principle applies for 32nd notes, 64th notes and so on. You cannot enter sixteenth notes if this setting is not 16 or higher.

If you wish to put your music on a regular grid, you use quantization. Quantization brings notes to their exact placement values. With the quantization set to 1/16, this means that if you played a sixteenth note a little early, the program will correct the note and move it to the exact placement of a sixteenth note.

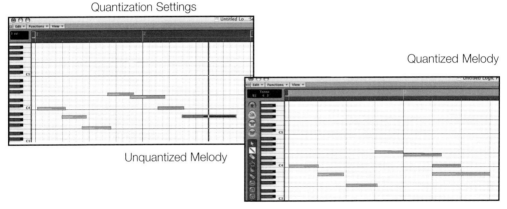

Quantization Settings

Quantized Melody

Unquantized Melody

Quantization then 'straightens out' time. If you set it to eighth notes, the program will move what you play to the nearest eighth note beat, for example. The same holds true for the other values. You can see this by playing a simple melody with 'record' on [⦿]] and then looking at the melody on the Matrix Screen.

But for now we will concentrate on getting the notes where you want them. If you misplace a note on the staff, you just click on it and drag it until it is where you want it to be. It is easier to place notes correctly when the staff is larger and the lines are farther apart. In the Score Screen you can also enlarge your staff by moving the slider or clicking the big side of the right enlargement telescope at the top right of the Score Screen. Alternatively, you can use 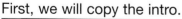 . The staves should have gotten bigger. Click again, and then again. With each click the staff is bigger and more accessible to note placement. You can do the opposite and diminish the screen by using . If you use a mouse with a wheel you can diminish and enlarge with Alt and wheel movements or by the key commands Ctl and the up and down Arrows.

Go back to the Score Screen and if any marks or notes are on it, erase them by selecting them and then deleting them with the backspace key.

Making the Lead Sheet

Intro	**0 - 11**
A	12 - 19
B	20 - 27
A	28 - 35
B'	36 - 42

Structure of 'Again'

You have printed the lead sheet for 'Again'. Take a close look at it. We are going to copy it. It has the general structure: Intro A B A B'. This means that the two A sections are identical and the B and B' sections are similar; at least similar enough to share the same letter. This means we can copy the first A section to the second unchanged, and the first B section to the second with revisions.

So far you have a work sheet in Logic with one instrument called voice and a blank staff of 30 bars. It has placed the treble clef according to the usual clef of the instrument and 4/4 time. You would select another time signature if you were not going to work in 4/4.

First, we will copy the intro.

Study the score looking for identical and similar measures. If the measures are identical or similar it is much easier to copy them as units than to copy them note by note from scratch. With the structure ABAB' we expect to copy whole A and B sections. If there is much difference between B and B' we will be adjusting the notes of B to that of B'. If there is more than one chorus, we will be copying lots of As and Bs. We will copy the intro note by note. The intro runs from the beginning through measure 11, disregarding for a moment the two notes of measure 11 which are really an upbeat to A which begins at measure 12. There is a lot of copying in arranging. Perhaps you will copy the A many times; from one chorus of A to another or from one section of A to the A of another instrument or group of instruments–in any case the basic melody will still have to be copied.

Open the Score Screen and select the eighth note symbol at the left of the screen. The first note of the lead sheet is C, an eighth note placed on the second part of beat three. Use the pencil with the mouse to place the note on the staff. The following notes are eighth notes so you do not have to reselect your note value. Place those notes on the staff as well. Do the same with the second measure. In the third measure you will have to reselect the note values, first to a quarter note, half note and eighth note. You will soon learn to copy all your notes of one value at a time. Since the eighth note is the predominant value, copy all of the eighth notes first, then the quarter notes, then the half notes. Copy the whole introduction.

It may sound patronizing to say so, but be sure to save frequently with ⌘+S in case the program quits suddenly or your dog pulls the electric cord out. These things can and do happen to the savviest of software users so saving regularly is an essential part of good work practice.

Identical and Similar Measures

Similar Measures

Copy the first A. Note which measures are identical. Measures 11, 13, and 15 are similar in note length (note value). We can copy them measure by measure. Unfortunately, the notes in measures 12 and 14 are similar but have different values. We will learn how to take advantage of this shortly, but for now we will copy those measures note by note. Here goes: copy bar 11 note for note then, holding down the Alt key and selecting all of the notes of the bar, drag them to bar 13. Adjust the pitches by clicking on the notes you want to adjust and move them. Be careful not to hold down the pencil or you will create notes. You do not wish to make a new note, just adjust a previous one.

Now, select the notes of measure 11, press ⌷alt⌷ and drag and copy those notes to measure 15. This is called drag-copying and we can select and copy several measures together. You will improve with practice. Copy bar 16. Select the triple quarter notes of measure 16 and then copy this triplet to measure 17 and then adjust it. Go back and complete measure 16, then measure 17.

Similar Measures

Go on copying to measure 19. Note that the tied half notes can be created by selecting and placing a whole note on beat three. The note will project into bar 19. Note that bars 19 through 22 are the same in note values to bars 23 to 25. Copy bars 19 through 22. Select those bars and, depressing the Alt key, drag-copy those bars to bars 23 to 25. Leave the notes in bars 23 to 25 selected. They will show that they are selected by blinking. Using your pointer, carefully adjust the pitch downward one half step. You will have to adjust a few notes, but most of the notes will be at the correct pitches. Then correct the incorrect pitches.

An Easier Way

This method is fine for a few notes but tiresome for longer work. Fortunately there is an easier way. It is possible to select your note value without having to move the mouse across the page to the partbox and to select the desired note value. If you keep the pencil pointer always on the staff the process becomes much easier. For example, if you knew that the note value of quarter, half, eighth, etc. was already selected, you would just have to worry about placing it where you want it on the correct staff. Easy to do!

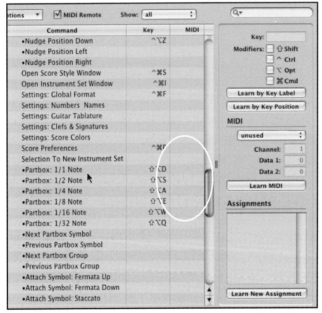

Create a key command in the Score Screen section of the Key Command Screen. In Logic 7 there is a table of contents. If it is not present because the key commands are expanded, choose 'options' and then 'collapse all'. Go to the section, 'Score Window', then to the section that assigns commands to note values called the 'Part box'.

Key Command for Note Values

The current Logic Pro 7 has two ways of learning and two different learn keys: by key designation or what is written on the key; and by key position on any keyboard. In the former, if the '?' is on the bottom row on the American keyboard but in the top numeric row on the International Spanish keyboard, the key with the symbol '?' will effect the same command. By key position, if key one right bottom row opens the instrument set box, then it will always open the instrument set box no matter what is written on the key. The learn by key position is the 'fit the hand' method where you remember by muscle memory rather than by what is written on the key.

You are still at Partbox 1/1 of the Score Screen section that says Part box 1/1 note. Click on it. The line you are on is darkened. With a 'learn key' turned on, press ⇧ + alt ⌥ + D simultaneously. You have now made a key command. Every time you press those keys and then pencil-click on a staff you will create a whole note. If you have the most recent Logic, use 'Learn by key label. Do the same with the other note values, creating command keys as follows:

half   =
quarter   =
eighth   =
sixteenth   =
thirty-second   =

Then turn off the learn key. Exit the Command Screen.

You now have the Key Command note values arranged as shown. You are using ⇧ + alt ⌥ with each command to make the commands for note values similar and familiar to the hand, and arranging the note values from small to large. Remember this when you are making up your own key commands; try and create them in meaningful groups of commands which will be easier to remember.

Enter a few bars using the key commands. You key in the value of a note and place and locate that note on the staff with the pencil tool. Then you repeat the process.

Press the eighth note command twice and look at the notes in the partbox. The triplet eighth is highlighted. If you press the eighth note again the dotted value is selected. The values rotate among these three possibilities for each note value. You will gain considerable speed through practice.

The rest of this chapter will show you easier ways to copy and input other data, and important and common techniques for inputting and aligning lyrics and other text. So take a deep breath and forge on. You are almost finished!

Easier Yet

So far so good; but you must still take pains with the locating of the note on the staff. Correcting misplacement of notes is tedious and time consuming. Assigning more Key Commands is the best way to combat this. Call up the Key Command Screen and find the command 'select previous event'. Assign this to the left arrow key. Assign 'select next event' to the right arrow key (or to any pair of easily remembered keys). Remember that other key assignments will be erased automatically. Not to worry; if the key is already assigned the program will tell you so. This command will move you from note to note, forwards or backwards.

Here is where the higher priced programs differ from the more economical (the higher price programs are Gold, Platinum and Logic Pro). The more costly programs enable the user to 'nudge' or move the notes one semitone at a time. If you have this capability, continue in this way to make the following assignments: [alt]+[↑] for 'transpose event +1' and [alt]+[↓] for 'transpose event - 1'. This will correct the pitch of notes.

In the more costly versions, also assign [ctrl]+[→] for 'nudge event position by beat + 1' and [ctrl]+[←] for 'nudge event position by beat - 1'. This moves the score forward or backward by the note duration value selected. In other words, if you want a phrase to start on beat four instead of beat three, select a quarter note on beat three and press [ctrl]+[→] once; to move another beat, press the command again.

If you do not have these versions you will have to change pitch with the Logic arrow tool only. This tool is slightly harder to work with than the command keys but is just as effective. If you have MIDI 'OUT' selected on the Score Screen, you will hear the note and the note changes which will help you in correcting the notes. Enlarging the staves and notes will also help visually in note placement with this tool.

Notice that these key commands are in the form of a compass, with the command to go up on top, down on the bottom, left on the left, etc. You now have a very powerful note inputting system at your command.

Select the first note of measure 1. Use [alt] + [↑] or the Logic arrow tool. The note should be raised a half step with each pressing of the key. If you are using the arrow tool you select the note by clicking, then grab it and move it upwards. Try the down arrow. If you miss the correct note positions when you are inputting quickly, you can go back and make quick corrections. To get to the notes to be changed click on any note or use the [←] + [→] arrow keys to get to the note you desire. You can even play the melody back as you go along by depressing the right arrow key; a quick way of checking errors. Make sure the 'OUT' button at top left has been illuminated (selected) so that you hear the notes.

Some other note corrections that you might want to make are changing sharps to flats and vice versa. The existing (pre-programmed) commands are [⇧] + [#] and [⇧] + [B] .

Make these two other useful commands for lengthening and shortening the duration of a note. Assign [⌘] + [→] to 'nudge' length by 'beat +1' and [⌘] + [←] 'nudge' length by 'beat -1'. These are 'nudge' commands and will only work with the more costly versions.

Copy the rest of the melody (the notes–not the chords or lyrics) onto the voice staff using your new found skills with the command keys. Good work! A lot easier than when you started, I hope.

One final task. Click on the page symbol in order to add the final editing touches. Click on the text icon [A] in the partbox and then on 'text', then on the header of the Score Screen where you want to put the title. As with notes, either the pencil or the text tool is used for entering. Enter the title and click again (elsewhere) to deselect the text you have entered. In the parameter box you can change and enlarge the font and, using the align symbols [⊣ ⊢], can place it on the page as you desire. For example, you could place your copyright notice at the left margin and the name of the composer at the right margin. You have to find the copyright command [©] on your own keyboard. Using a British or American Mac keyboard it is usually Alt + G, European Keyboard Alt + C.

Next we will add lyrics and chords to the lead sheet and learn two other ways to input the melody.

Changing between Screens

This will save you a good bit of time. In Key Commands you have a list of all of the windows. The program refers to the screens (also called editors) as 'Windows'. You are familiar with several of them. The Key Commands for the screens 1 – 9 are pre-programmed. They are all of the basic screens that you see in the menu >Windows.

If you make use of other screensets, perhaps multiple screens, you use numbers plus ⇧ . Make the screens as large as you want them, then press ⇧ +L (pre-assigned) to lock them in. You can unlock the screens with ⇧ +L . Try to make screenset numbers that are easy to remember. A temporary written list that you keep by the screen will help.

You can have up to 99 different screens. The number of screensets may seem excessive (99), but when working on a big band arrangement, using many screens can be a big time saver.

Lyrics

Click the text icon in the part box, the symbol that looks like an 'A'. A further choice is offered to you of text, lyric, chord etc. Choose lyric. Make sure you use the pencil pointer and that you click on the choice 'lyric' with it. Go to where you want the first word of the lyric to be and click. A vertical bar appears. Type in the first word and pause.

You can type a word or a syllable, then press the tab key, and you will be advanced to the next division value that is set in the Transport Bar. The value '2' stands for the division of a half note, '4' stands for a quarter note, '1/16' for a sixteenth note. If you do not want to place a word or syllable where the cursor has left you, press the tab key again and you will be moved along to the next division. To end the string of lyric inputs click or press enter.

If you mistakenly entered a wrong word or syllable somewhere, at any time select it and delete it, or, double-click on it and correct the flashing entry just as you correct the text on your word processor.

Make sure the page mode key is not illuminated in Score. You will find it more convenient to work in staff mode (staves horizontal) than in page mode, except when you are printing.

Aligning Lyrics, Chords and Text

Returning to the task at hand, if you want to align the lyrics vertically or move them lower or higher on the staff away from the notes, select the first lyric of the first line of lyrics and 'select all similar' from the edit menu. Do not choose 'select all', or you will literally get all and make undesired changes. This makes all the selected lyrics in the score blink. Change the number of 'Vertical Pos.' in the parameter box. Not only will the text be moved up or down, it will be aligned perfectly. If you just want to align a few words, group select them and align in the same way and then align the rest by eye or repeat the process.

Since you are not in full page mode, you can easily scroll horizontally from start to finish of your song to ensure that the lyric is vertically straight. Use the scroll icon at the bottom of the screen, or the scroll wheel together with

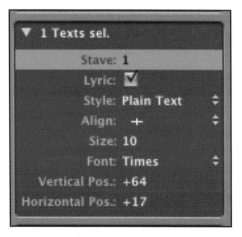

[if you have a scroll wheel on your mouse].

You can select the type, font and size of your lyrics at any time by selecting >Text >Text Styles and changing the fonts and effects (underscoring, italics, bolding). You can follow a similar process to align your copyright notice and credits in the header.

Chords

We will now follow basically the same process with entering chord symbols. Choose the text icon and the 'chord' option. Pencil-click where you want the first chord to go. Enter chord symbol 'C7' at the vertical marker and then press the tab key. The chord will have been registered and the vertical marker moved to the spot above the next displayed note or rest. Press tab again, and the vertical marker moves to the next quarter note, where you might want to enter the next chord.

If you have to construct a particularly complicated chord you may click on part of the chord to correct or enter your text.

A huge time-saving tip here: if you are entering mostly one chord per bar, enter your chords on an empty sequence. The tab key will advance the cursor to the next bar, making one chord entry per bar move along very rapidly. You can copy the finished chords to the appropriate staff afterwards.

You should read about the conventions of describing chords. There are different styles of usage: German, American, Jazz, Classical. Basically, dealing with chords is the same as with lyrics. You can align, raise, lower or correct chords in the same way.

Text

Choose the text option now. Enter rubato and other expression terms. Like the font? If not, change it. I like to make the font for expression words different from the font for instruction words. You can change the type, font and size in the parameter box or with the menu choice text. The menu option can be set and forgotten, the parameter box only deals with selected text. Choose your text styles on the Score Screen with the menu choice >Text >Text Styles. The text function was upgraded in version 7, and there are a lot of fonts and styles (called 'faces') available.

Other Score Symbols

This is a good opportunity to learn and experiment with other part box icons such as staccato, fermata, jazz symbols, inputting crescendos and decrescendos, dynamic markers, double bars to delineate sections and final double bars. Remember that double bars for returns are for the eyes only and do not make the program play them.

Once again this is a good place to remind you to save your work frequently (⌘+s or Menu >File >Save). I keep different versions of my arrangements in progress with dates incorporated into their filenames as temporary files. You will develop your own system.

Getting around the staves

Clicking on the lowest part of the ruler near the barline will get you to a particular measure. When you do not have a clear view of the destination bar you want to go to but know the bar number, press 'G' and type in the bar number.

Undo and Revert to Saved

The later versions of Logic have an undo function which allows you to remove your work command by command with ⌘+z until you get back to where you took a wrong turn.   If you remember that you took a false step three steps ago, you can get back to that point by pressing the same command three times. If you have been working for a while and then decide to remove most of the work, it is an easier option to choose >File >Revert to Save. This has the same effect as quitting the song without saving and then opening it again.

More Ways to Input

Inputting from the screen.

This will make your arranging even easier. You can already input by writing notes to the staff with your pencil key. This method is called step inputting with your keyboard (synth), and there is a section on inputting with Logic's built-in piano keyboard. They can be used for inputting together or separately. A large part of your printed arrangement will be done using step inputting.

Make sure you have selected the track of the MIDI instrument you are inputting to. Go back to the point where you have your Score Screen in front of you with a staff at least 30 bars long.

Call up the Key Command Screen. Find the section called 'Keyboard Input', and in that section the different note values. Enter the same commands for the same note values that you did in the score section, your now familiar pattern of QWE/ASD. Remember, you will see that the same key command in different screens can have different meanings. Not to worry. Right now we are just interested in the meaning of the key commands in the keyboard entry section of the Key Command Screen. You will now be able to select the value of your note with your key commands or by choosing them on the part box on the screen.

Step Input - Method 1

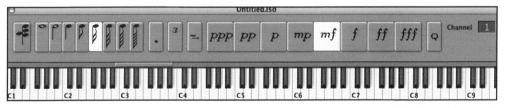

Step Input Keyboard

Open the Logic keyboard with >Windows >Step Input Keyboard. You can use the Logic keyboard alone, selecting the note values from the keyboard and putting the notes on the staff by clicking on the keys of the keyboard.

Step Input - Method 2

You can do the same but write the notes to the staff by playing the keys of your synthesizer. On the top left of the screen next to the OUT icon box is an IN icon box. Click it on. This will record your keyboard.

Step Input   - Method 3

You can do the same but write the notes to the staff by using the command keys for the note values and playing them on the staff with your synthesizer. This does not use the Logic keyboard at all.

You can see that step inputting is a very flexible system. Do not forget to click the IN button. The program writes the notes at the position of the SPL, which is automatically advanced to the next note.

The Caplock Keyboard

Caplock Keyboard

The possibility exists for using the computer's keyboard or a representation of a keyboard (turned on and off in Score by the Caplock key). Notes are assigned to the keys in the form of an octave on a keyboard. The uppermost keys are used to change the octave. It is devilishly clever and useful on a laptop in an airplane when one doesn't have a keyboard at hand.

You can play chords without pressing the chord key of the step input keyboard. You will be able to write for several instruments by splitting the chords into parts, line by line as you go. This will enable you to write for an entire section all at once.

Enter more of the melody for some practice with step inputting to get comfortable with it. Then we move on to another method, the recording method. Remember, set quantization to the smallest note division value of the score; if you are going to be writing sixteenth notes, set it to sixteenths.

Live or Recording Input

The recording method consists of playing the melody on your synthesizer. It does not matter if you are not the greatest keyboardist. You can just record at a very slow tempo. You can also correct the score easily with your note movement Key Commands. If you are working with a PC do not use the arrow keys for key commands: unfortunately, the program already uses some of these combinations to manage the menus. Setting up these commands with Alt + arrows causes confusion and will get you tangled up in the menus. Set up a cross on P,L,>,and ' in conjunction with the Alt and Ctl keys instead.

Open the Arrange Screen. Change the recording tempo according to your keyboard skills by clicking and dragging the time number on the Transport Bar. Select the track (not the sequence) that you wish to record (easy, you only have one instrument track) and then click on the record button on the Transport Bar or find the key command for record. I recommend it being assigned to keypad ⟨*⟩ . If it is not assigned, do so now. You assign it in the 'Global Commands' section of the Key Command Screen. Commands in that section are used throughout the program; you cannot use one command in a different section with a different meaning.

The metronome should start clicking when you press record. If not, go first to >File >Song Settings >Metronome (or reach it by clicking ⟨icon⟩ on the Transport Bar, then choosing 'Metronome') to make sure that the appropriate boxes are checked. You have the choice of playing the metronome through your computer speaker or through your built-in speakers. You also have the choice of using 'Klopfgeist' an audio-instrument, on audio-instrument track 64.

If there are still problems open the Environment Screen and add a metronome by menu choosing New and then MIDI metronome. Now click and hold on the metronome icon on the Transport Bar, [ ] then choose 'Metronome'. Make sure the channel setting is the channel for an existing drum kit (in Environment as an instrument). In a drum kit, single notes of the scale represent congas, wood blocks, snare drums, toms, bass drums, cymbals, high hats, etc. Set the drum notes for the sounds you desire. Close the box again on the metronome icon and go to 'metronome'. Click the boxes for 'click while recording' and 'MIDI metronome'. Go to the recording box to set the number of bars to click you in before the recording starts. I prefer a one bar click in but it is a very subjective choice. Close the box. Press record to test the metronome.

You should still be in the Arrange Screen. If something has gotten recorded in the track while you were experimenting, select it and delete. Move the Song Position Line to the bar on which you wish to begin recording. An extremely handy way to do this is to make key commands that advance or send back the SPL one bar at a time. These are among the most useful key commands you will have at your disposal. Assign the ']' to move the SPL forward and '[' to move it backwards.

Now press record, wait for the click, and then play eight bars of the melody. Press stop (the space bar) and reset back to bar one (keypad 0) for 'rewind to bar 1'. You can see when the SPL moves to bar one, beat one. Press play and listen. If you goofed up the recording, you can delete it in the Arrange Screen and go back to bar one and record again and again. Check the score of your recording by moving to the Score Screen. When you want to record further, position the SPL to where you want to start recording.

You can do this in many ways, depending on which screen you are in. If you are in the Score Screen, find the bar you wish to start from, press record, and click on the bar. If the running man icons are clicked on in the Arrange and Score Screens, when you now go to the Arrange Screen the SPL will be in the same position on both screens. When the running man is illuminated, the SPL is always visible. It moves from bar to bar as the song plays. You can repeat the playing in of the melody at any location with this recording technique as often as needed.

Finish copying 'Again'.

Printing

Print your new, just completed version of 'Again' even though you already have a copy. You should have the practice of printing when it does not count, when you do not have to immediately present parts or a lead sheet.

When you have the song as you want it, put it in page mode and check it again. You may want to adjust the height of the top and bottom margins. An easy way is to click and hold on the clef of the first staff and drag it up or down. This adjusts the whole song. After each readjustment of the first clef on the first staff, scroll through the other pages to see how the print set up was affected, diminishing the view with Alt + the scroll wheel, slider or the telescope. You do this to see a print preview. Precise margin settings can be made from >Menu >File >Song Settings >Score: General; or in older versions by searching out 'Global Format'. Alternatively you can set the margins by grabbing and dragging with the arrow as long as the 'Print View' is enabled. You can get to the same menu choice by clicking the metronome on the transport bar and choosing Recording Options then Score. When the margins are where you want them to be, print it out using 'Print' in the File menu or ⌘+p .

We will talk more about printing later on, when you need to print players' parts and a conductor's score.

Now that you know how to create a staff and enter a melody, enter the lyrics and chords and print a lead sheet, we will move on to working with many staves and many instruments.

Making a Score Template

A time saving tip here and a real arranging tool: the Score Template.

Boot Logic. Open a new song. Your 'Autoload. Iso' will be loaded. It has three kinds of tracks: MIDI, audio and virtual instrument tracks. So that we are all working on the same thing, we will enter the following instrument, pan, and volume settings on these channels, using MIDI instruments for our example, and specify the General MIDI program. You will be changing or adding to the instruments, but this is a good place to start.

Channel	instrument	vol	pan
1	clarinet	60	115
2	trumpet	50	95
3	tuba	30	75
4	guitar	30	45
10	drums	35	25

Open the Score Screen. There are no notes or staves in the score. Instruments are there on the tracks on the Arrange Screen and in the Environment, and no staves set up for the instruments. After you have entered the instruments as directed, save them with 'Save Templates' Save this under the name 'Combo'. You can do this with virtual instruments in the same manner but make sure you save the template with the instruments in place and the samples loaded.

You have made what is called a 'Score Template' or 'Score Set-up' for a combo. It is easier to start a combo or other small arrangement from here than from scratch. You will have a file called 'Combo Template' with nothing in it but instruments! You can make other Score Templates like Big Band or String Quartet. If you want to create a Salsa Combo with loads of percussion, start out with the Combo Template and then add the percussion instruments you need. Make sure to save your template under that name.

As with so much in Logic, you can do the same task in many different ways. Here is another way to create the Combo Template. With 'Hotcha!' loaded, open the Arrange Screen. Then select all of the extraneous tracks with the arrow and delete them. To create the same blank Combo Template you will have to erase the staves. Get the SPL back to the beginning of bar one and erase each staff by selecting it and backspacing.

Use whichever method you find easiest. I prefer the first method rather than erasing existing songs because I do not always remember what I did before to the song. I worry that I did not erase everything – that there could be something left over in the environment or elsewhere.

We are now ready to go to work. You can also save this song with 'Save Template'. Use the method that you are comfortable with.

The Plan

We are going to copy Hotcha! The assignment was to create film music for an ambulatory Dixieland band of about 1910. This is my version. Copy or tear out the song 'Hotcha' in the Appendix. Read or play through the score a few times for familiarity. Play the melody through a few more times on a keyboard, adding some harmony. Think about how you would arrange it. Which instruments would you use? Of the two main instruments, which plays the lead, which plays the second? Do they switch roles? What about the ranges–of each instrument? Listen to the CD. Do you agree with the arranger's decisions?

Notice how strong two instruments sound when playing in unison. Conventionally, when two lines are playing solo the distance between the notes is usually nil (unison), a third or a sixth (major or minor). Did you notice how the piece started in unison, went to two voices, and ended in unison? Do you notice how voices are added, and the effect that this has on the listener?

It is a good idea to write out a plan for your arrangement with groups of bars that show: which instrument(s) are used melody and which as accompaniment; tempo; dynamics; ideas for counter-melodies, embellishments; or other arranging choices like instrumentation or voicings. Establish the climax point and think how to lead up to it. Indicate the overall dynamic plan, that is, crescendi and diminuendi, pp and fff. Time spent on the plan will more than be made up in the actual writing. You get a picture of the entire arrangement and can pay attention to important concepts like density of instrumentation, dynamics and harmonic rhythm.

I have developed a sketch that shows many aspects of an arrangement:

Instrument	Name of Instrument
Number	How many of each instrument
Used as	Melody
Style	Type of ensemble
Architecture	Size of ensemble
Special Effects	Unison, combinations of instruments
Volume	
Pan	
Acoustic effect 1	
Acoustic effect 2	
Acoustic effect 3	
Beat	How many beats per bar
Overall	
Dynamics	Does the volume change? Does the band move?
Speed	Tempo, does it change?
Comments	

You may repeat the instrument section for all of the lead or accompaniment instruments as well as any solo instruments. 'Used as' is how the instruments are used. You do not have to comment on everything. If there is little to say about bass and drum, merely indicate them. If the piano is used as accompaniment just say so and no more; you do not have to think too long about the number of pianos you want in your ambulatory band. Our solo instruments are indicated and whether or not they are accompanied or unison. After you have put down something once you do not have to repeat it, just say that there is one trumpet and one clarinet and that it is a small band; you only have to fill in that category again if you change the size or nature of the group. Here is a chorus-by-chorus sketch of 'Hotcha!', especially showing the two lead, small combo instrumentation and who plays what (lead, accompaniment, obligato, background figures). 'Beat' refers to beats per bar, the percussive 'feel' of walking bass or four-beat drums; a quarter note means 4 beats per bar, a half note means two beats per bar. This is far from all-inclusive, but it gives you an idea of the complexity of an arrangement and is a useful guide to a preliminary sketch. The musical sign for 'repeat' [./.] , is used for 'continues to be played as...'.

Rather than only dividing the instruments into 'melody' and 'accompanying' instruments I have used the term 'secondary' instrument for one that is playing at the same time as a lead instrument but is more than mere accompaniment. The two instruments are playing a third or a sixth or a third apart, and in soli, that is, with the same time values per note but different pitches. The Guitar, provides rhythm and harmony but since it does not contribute to the melody, it is, to me, 'accompaniment'.

You may make the chart larger. Sometimes a single sketch is better at showing the dynamic curve or the approach to the climax. Sometimes colored pencils are a help in showing lead-second alternation on your chart.

	A	A	B	A
		Chorus 1		
Instrument				
Name of Instrument	Trumpet-	⁒	⁒	⁒
Number	1			
Used	Melody (unison)			
Style	1910 Jazz -			
Architecture	Combo			
Special Effects	2 leads unison			
Volume	60			
Pan	10			
Acoustic effect 1	Reverb			
Acoustic effect 2				
Beat				
Instrument				
Name of instrument	Clarinet	⁒	⁒	⁒
Number	1			
Used as	Melody secondary (unison)			
Style	1910 jazz			
Architecture	Combo			
Special Effects	2 Leads unison			
Volume	80			
Pan	20			
Acoustic effect 1	Reverb			
Acoustic effect 2				
Beat				
Instrument				
Name of instrument	Banjo	⁒	⁒	⁒
Number	1			
Used as	ACC			
Style	1910 Jazz			
Architecture	Combo			
Special Effects	Strum w/ pick			
Volume	40			
Pan	0			
Acoustic effect 1	Reverb			
Acoustic effect 2				
Beat	4/bar			
Overall				
Dynamics				
Speed	95			
Comment				

Copying

We are first going to copy the song in many different ways. Usually we copy or play in the melody lines of each instrument, then add the second line. Hotcha! is an AABA song, a structure that was common throughout the twentieth century and today. AABA refers to the structure. The eight bar A sections are almost alike, the B section is the bridge, and another eight bar A section ends the first chorus. Actually the piece has five complete choruses. The possibilities of structure allow an introduction and addition of an interlude of anywhere from eight to thirty-two bars after the second or third chorus. I have added neither. Instead I have chosen to put little solos in the main body of the work. I consider that it has made the arrangement sufficiently interesting. The song begins and ends with mostly unison choruses. The song ends with tags, which are phrases usually reminiscent of the rest of the song, played over and over. Look at the sketch again to see the AABA structure.

You can load several songs at once and work on each one, copying from one song to another, in the same Logic session.

Method 1 Playing in

Go to the arrange screen. You should have no staves anywhere. Set your metronome to a tempo you can control (do not be shy about using slow tempi). Press record. You hear your metronome lead-in (I set this to one measure). Play measure 1-16 in the clarinet. Bring the SPL to 0 with keypad 0 or with two presses of the stop button on the Transport Bar, select trumpet and record again. This time you can hear the clarinet, which you have already recorded, playing along. Since you want the instruments to play in unison, you leave the clarinet sounding (you have the choice of muting the clarinet by selecting the 'M' on the track). You have just recorded the bridge on both instruments, measures 9 – 16. You can do the same for measures 25 – 32, or since these measures are the same as measures 9 – 16, you can copy the notes by playing them in or with the other methods just about to be discussed. Read on. If you like this method, you can copy all of the choruses this way.

Play the melody in with record, using the command keys or pointer for note and pitch correction, if necessary. If your music is to be presented live you should use the play-in method as much as possible. Played-in music sounds much more natural than mouse entered music. When you later copy short pieces of played in melody it does not lose its 'played-in' sound, even if repeated many times. Start out by copying one chorus at a time.

'Chorus' refers to a repetition of an AABA section. The B section is often referred to as the 'bridge'. The introduction is called the 'intro' or the 'verse'. These terms are commonly used by musicians. Some musicians use the term 'verse' to mean the bit of lyrics that appears in contrast to the term 'chorus'. To avoid confusion, I tend to avoid the use of the term 'verse', and only use 'chorus' to mean an entire AABA or ABAB of a song.

Method 2

As usual with Logic there is more than one way to copy. This assumes that you are making a part for printing, not for playing. This method is a traditional cut and paste method. Create a staff in Arrange of 40 measures. Mouse in measures 1-8 (or play them in and lengthen the staff afterwards). Make an empty staff of 40 measures to put notes on in the trumpet part. Select bars 1 through 8 of the clarinet part. Press ⌘+c (already programmed in your Key Commands), move to the clipboard command. Move the SPL by command-clicking the beat and bar that you want to move to or by using the [+] to bar 9, still on the clarinet staff. Make sure that you are exactly on the beat of the bar of the staff that you desire to copy to. You can check if the SPL is correctly positioned (at the beginning of the beat) by checking the top address box on the Transport Bar. If you want the first beat of bar 9, this address should read 9 1 1 1. If you are not right on, you can centre the bar by advancing the SPL one bar with the [, and then moving backwards with the] . Highlight the clarinet staff by clicking on it. Now press ⌘+v , the paste command. The melody should appear, blinking. Click (elsewhere) to deselect the staff. Go to measure 18 and correct the melody to agree with the printed lead sheet. Now rubber band select all of the clarinet notes in measures 1-16. ⌘+c them and move to measure 1 of the trumpet staff.

Make sure that the SPL is located at 1111. Now use ⌘+v , and you have the unison melody in the trumpet, too. You can use the correcting key commands or pointer to correct the pitch if you have to. The use of the brackets moves you bar for bar through the song, stopping, when necessary, for correction.

Continue in the same way for the bridge. After you have moused in the clarinet's bars 17-24, copy them to the trumpet part. Keep the new notes of the trumpet selected (they are blinking), grab one of the notes with the arrow, and move them a third lower than the clarinet. Those of you who have pitch key commands could have easily done this with Key Commands. Or you could have corrected the pitch with your mouse. Correct the pitch of the trumpet to make a perfect duet.

Now, in the same way, move the SPL to the first beat of the clarinet's measure 25. Select bars 1-8 of the clarinet; press Command C, then Command V. Correct the last measure.

Method 3

This method is similar to method 2, but instead of cut and paste you are going to select the notes you want to copy and drag them with the pointer to where you want them to be copied. Still in the Score Screen and holding down the Alt key, drag-copy everything in exactly the same sequence.

Method 4

This is quickest of all. Copy, as above, the clarinet's bars 1-16. In the Arrange Screen Alt drag this to create identical trumpet part of 16 bars. Correct it as above. Create bars 17-24 in clarinet (in the Score Screen). Go back to Arrange and Alt drag this to the trumpet's 17-24. Voila! A chorus. The difference in Methods 3 and 4 is that in 3 you drag-copy notes, in 4 you drag-copy sequences.

Soli Writing

Soli style is often used with two voices. Soli writing is an important concept. It means that all of the instruments comprising a section play the same rhythm but with harmony, as seen in this song. The 'section' can be the sax section or in the case of a combo, two or three instruments.

We are working with soli in this song. That is why the duet in bars 17-24 was so easy to correct.

Two Voices

Go to bar 25 1 1 1. Select the trumpet staff. Copy bars 1-8 of the trumpet staff using one of the methods. Copy it to the staff of the clarinet. Copy trumpet 25-32 to clarinet 25-32. Go back to the trumpet line. The two lines are soli. You have to adjust the pitches of the trumpet in the second line. When writing soli the rhythm of both lines is identical. It is less time consuming without having to enter note values.

To finish the chorus you must add the tuba line and the percussion. We can write the tuba part with the mouse. The different bars of the guitar part can be played in and then cut and pasted into place. A few bars of the drum part can be played in and then repeated. Place the drum part in bar one. Press the R key and enter. A little rectangle comes up asking you how many bars you wish to repeat. Type '31'. You have now finished the first chorus.

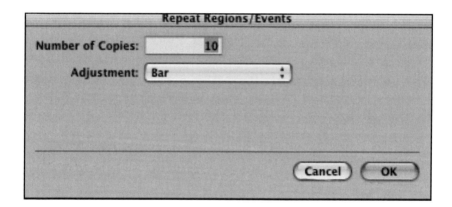

Copy a few choruses. This time you can copy all five staves at once by rubber banding and then correcting them. If you have any trouble with this, copy the clarinet, bars 1 – 32, then the trumpet, bars 1 – 32 etc.

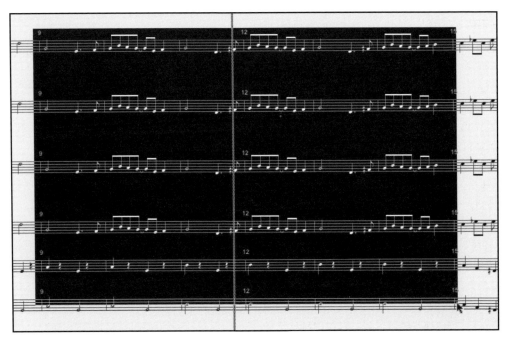

Selecting Several Staves at Once

More Ways to Copy

The use of R, above, is another, albeit limited, way of copying. It is useful for copying short phrases. Keep it in your inventory of ways to copy and use it interchangeably with the other methods. Because it sounds too perfect and hence mechanical, it should not be used for lead instruments (without modification). We will deal with this at length in future chapters.

As we have seen, this method of repeating is useful for creating percussion and bass parts. Record or write a measure or two of repetitive high hat or cymbal then repeat until the end of the song or a different rhythm. To liven up the percussion and to avoid monotony use your movement keys to go through the part making occasional changes to the basic pattern. You could use the 'loop' command to repeat a drum part but you can make no interventions in it to make it sound more human and less mechanical. Try entering a bar in the drum staff, then press loop in the top left of the Arrange Screen, or draw out the staff from above the mid-point with the loop bar creating tool [ ].

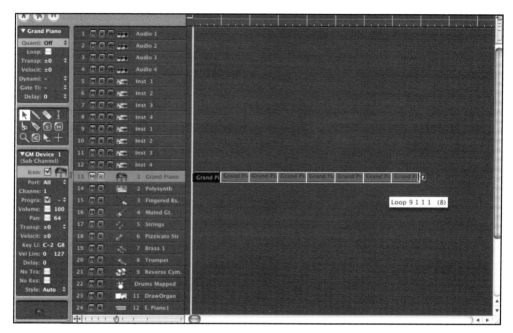

Loop on Arrange Screen

When creating walking bass parts I often repeat a measure of quarter notes 10 or 20 times and then advance through it making changes with my movement keys or with the mouse. First I write the basic walking part and then I jazz it up with another pass.

You can have a song containing an inventory of parts to be copied, for example walking bass, or violin runs of 16th notes without having to build the part from scratch. It will come in handy. You can copy from another song with cut and paste.

What is important is that you have learned to copy a melody in the most efficient way for the situation, and to copy or repeat phrases. There are refinements to Logic's copy process. One can insert and replace copy in different ways or switch the locations of the copies. I have never used them. Maybe I am too much of the school 'If it ain't broke, don't fix it' but straightforward copying works so well I have never found a reason to change.

Another way to get to any bar and beat is to press G and enter where you want to go to.   You can go to any bar by clicking the bar at the point where the ruler meets the bar, or better yet, on the bar itself with Alt. Sometime, though, the bar is very distant and not visible.   That is when G comes in handy. An alternate method of moving where you want to go is to use the square brackets to move the SPL bar by bar.

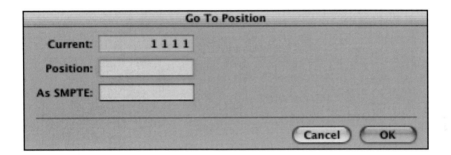

Setting up your Drums

Before anything, you want to see the percussion available to you. Open the Environment screen. Choose a drum instrument like GM drum. Place this instrument on a track of the Assign Screen with the channel and port assigned.   Play the keyboard and listen to which percussion instrument is assigned to which note.

Click the metronome on the Transport Bar, then 'Recording Options'. You make sure you can merge new recordings with existing recordings here. Select the drum track. Choose your favorite bass drum. Record it on beats 1 and 3. Go back to zero or put cycle on. Record your favorite snare on beats 2 and 4. Go back again and record a cymbal on beats 2 and 4.

You want to keep these instruments separate on the score sheet. Normally you are in percussion clef or bass clef on the Score Screen; I have put you in bass clef for more clarity. On the parameter bar of the Score Screen you see special symbols for heads of drum notes. Select the notes representing the bass drum, then >Edit >Select Similar Regions/Events.   Select the notehead you want for the bass drum. Touch the pencil to one of the notes and all of the notes receive the bass drum notehead. Now do the same for the snare drum's notes.

Drum Part

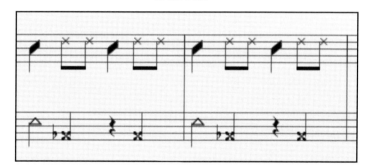

Same Part with Noteheads

You can make your own one or two measure drum patterns and elongate them by repeating with R or the loop tool. I would use R and create a variation every four or five bars to 'humanize' the drum part a bit. You can also 'play' the drums for the complete song and 'let your fingers do the walking' for real humanization.

Additional Work

I have included a little melody, similar in style to 'Hotcha!', for you to harmonize and arrange. It is written for the same instruments. Make a plan for five choruses then arrange it. In your writing use mostly thirds, sixths and unisons. Complete one chorus and copy all five staves with cut and paste as a starter for a second chorus. Be sure to save with   every once

in a while. Play what you copied. Does it sound good? Experiment with it.
You can go back and correct what does not sound right. Respect the style,
the 'feel' of the song. We are not writing hard bop or modal jazz, so keeping
the harmony simple will make it sound like the jazz of an earlier era.

Stay within the natural range of each instrument. A few notes at the bottom
and top of the instrument always sound different from the rest. An easy way
to know what are the good notes of an instrument: neither at the very bottom
nor top, but in the area that sounds typical of the instrument.

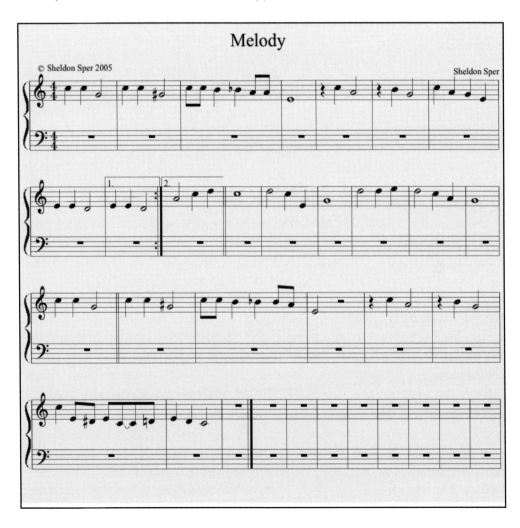

Chapter V:
Three Voices

Play 'I'm Flying and Feeling So Fine' on the CD a few times to get a feeling for the melody, since that is the song you are going to copy. The printed version is in the Appendix. We are going to make a medium combo arrangement of this theme. We will plan out the arrangement in advance, as we did for the exercise with two voices. First we choose the instruments and the accompaniment for the first chorus. 'Chorus' means one repetition of the complete melody, (AABA).

Of course we have to take into account why and for whom the arrangement is being made. We imagine a variety show, where one wants to showpiece a singer and also give a bit of a showcase to the musicians. Two and a half choruses will do (no bridge in the second chorus).

Make planning in advance a habit. It will save you a lot of time when it comes to actually writing. Arranging, in some respects, is a bit like computer programming. First the programmer writes a broad plan of what the program is to do, at which point, and how he is going to do it. Then he fills his plan in. Remember this analogy when you are arranging. Even though we are filling in a completed arrangement, look at the parameters of the arrangement sketch presented in the last chapter.

From your printout, fill in the sketch mentally: the lead instuments; who gets the solos and when they appear, etc. Still using the printout for guidance, open the Environment, select and place the instruments and their channels and bring them to the Arrange Screen.

In all band arrangements, small or large, the instruments are placed on the score sheet like this:

Big Band

alto sax,	1st	These players may also double on flute,
alto sax ,	2nd	clarinet or soprano sax so they go here
tenor sax,	1st	
tenor sax	2nd	
baritone sax		

trumpet,	1st	Trumpet also doubles with fluegel horns
trumpet,	2nd	
trumpet,	3rd	
trumpet,	4th	

trombone,	1st	
trombone,	2nd	
trombone,	3rd	
trombone,	4th	

guitar or piano	Sometimes guitar, sometimes piano,
bass	sometimes both
drums	

The size of the ensemble is expanded or contracted according to the need. A jingle may need more than five saxes or an oboe 'color' instrument. Usually the reed men double on other reed instruments, so you will get your oboes or clarinets, but not when those musicians are supposed to be playing sax. This order is always maintained, whether there are more or fewer instruments in the arrangement.

We are using two tenor saxophones in our arrangement plus the basic ensemble, plus bandoneon, which represents a singer. When you hear bandoneon, think singer.

INSTRUMENT	CHANNEL	
bandoneon	1	
tenor sax, 1st	2	
tenor sax, 2nd	3	
trumpet, 1st	4	
trombone, 1st	5	
piano	6	
bass	7	
drums	8	(10 in General MIDI)
voice	9	

Things to Keep in Mind

In many ways it is harder to write for a combo than for a big band. Firstly, there are fewer voices to convey the harmonies. You have to depend more on your piano or guitar for harmonic meaning (the actual chords). Then there is the richness of sound; in a big band you have section highlighting. For example, a great sound is a full sax section playing in close harmony accompanied by bass and drums. Or a call and response chorus between the brass and the saxes. Three instruments playing together can be as interesting and distinctive as a section of saxes or trombones playing harmony.

You can create interesting timbres by combining the instruments in different ways. When you have trumpet as soprano voice playing the melody on top, alto or tenor sax as second voice and trombone on the bottom, the trio of instruments produces a sound more like a brass section; whereas alto on top playing the melody, trumpet in the middle and trombone below sound more like a sax section. What is most important is that the combinations sound different and can be used to create contrast.

What makes up for the smaller numbers are greater solo possibilities, with many instruments having their say during a number. Another advantage is that you can have more choruses of the song than with a big band arrangement without creating boredom.

Knowing the structure of a piece in advance is a big help. You know the size of the units you will be using in copying the song. Most songs have a structure. Even lack of a recognizable structure is still a structural alternative.

In mainstream jazz, the usual structure of a piece is the first chorus with a recognizable theme, followed by choruses of solos based on the harmonies of the theme. The last chorus returns to the recognizable theme. Only occasionally, with a very well known theme, will the artist start with an improvisation on the theme – and then most people are in on the joke – and finally play the theme so that the less hip will catch on.

How Arrangers Think...

Here is how an arranger thinks: 'The first thing we do is make a choice of instruments and the sound we want to create.' This song is A1 A2 B A3, so each of these will be our segments. We especially want the Bs to contrast with the As. The first decision is the choice of instruments to be used: which for solo and which for accompaniment. What is the stucture of the arrangement? How many choruses? Intros and tags? Fast or slow? This pretty much decides the arrangement. The other details are added to the basic sketch.

'Rhythmic figures for the background, dynamics, where is the climax point, any changes of key?' Imagine how the arrangement sounds and how you make it so.

'The lyrics are important so the song cannot be played too fast. We want to speed up the chorus slightly because we are going to slow down for the tags and exit of the singer. We also want a stylized instrumental treatment of the melody.' For the melody, we will choose an instrument for its recognizable timbre. This will represent a singer. Following the first verse (the singer) we will have a Louis Armstrong style trumpet solo.

'Let us assign the sound type and harmony for each section, if we can, whether soli, lead-accompaniment, unison or counter-melody. The B section should be different from the A section (the instruments are changed to the clarinets, playing in their low register). There is repetition in the tag choruses.' [I believe that people like repetition. A popular theory is that people experience the same music in different ways every time they hear it. The first time they appreciate the novelty, the second time they appreciate the familiarity. Thinking this ways frees you to copy whole sections for re-use, which makes the piecing-together of the arrangment much easier.]

I always write my sketches in pencil, so I can insert changes. At this point everything is tentative. Any ideas for transitions and counter-melodies I jot down. Some counter-melodies are used more than once.

'Any other ideas such as accents, drum accompaniments, bass lines, stacato passages or the use of other expressive accents? What about the dynamics? Should I put the climax of the arrangement near the end?' [The climax is often louder and higher than anything that went before. Most arrangements build up to a climax, gradually increasing the tension and loudness until the big moment.]

'I think I will use use a walking bass throughout, a four beat constantly moving bass.'

On the bass staff make four measures of quarter notes. Use R and repeat 40 times for a quick template, then move the notes to where you want them with your key commands. We want a bass part at this early stage because the song will sound better having an accompaniment. Add a simple drum part here to give the song some movement. It will get your creative juices flowing.

Basses traditionally play the fundamental of the chord, scale step 1, alternating with scale step 5, sometimes with notes of the chord triad or with an ornamentation. In the printed score you see the melody in the trumpet and the chords in the piano part directly below as a guide. When you add the bass part live be sure to add some sixeenth notes before the beat which give the impression of a real bass being plucked.

Plucked Bass 1/2 note feel

Copy the spread, usually 1, 3 and 7 of the chord plus the bass part. Leave two empty staves for piano and drums. These players usually add their parts ad. lib. And you do not have to write them out. Very often the bass player makes his own part, unless you have special ideas for him to play, as is the case here.

Counter-melody

Another way of adding interest besides changing dynamics, timbre and instrument(s) is to add a second melody to contrast with the existing melody. This may come in the form of an added background figure or a complete melody. The only difference between a background figure (B.G.) and a countermelody is that the latter is continuous and of longer duration. You can use a counter-melody or B.G. figure alone and then in combination with the main melody, or use the two together right away. Ample examples of both are given in the songs.

Counter-melody

Background

Copying

I don't want you to misunderstand me. Between this discussion and my insistance on a sketch you might think I have a rather mechanical approach to arranging. Nothing could be further from the truth. But I value a disciplined approach at the right time and recognize the value of repetition.

There is a lot of copying in arranging. Classical players see this in orchestral scores. Anyone who has played dance band arrangements has returns where he plays the same lines over several choruses while the lead instruments change. The makes the arrangement easier to learn and to play, but provides enough variety to provide interest.

Building the Arrangement

You can see that there is still a lot of Logic to learn through copying an existing arrangement before you make an arrangement of your own. We will refer to the printed 'Flying', when we copy it. You know that it has the structure A1 A2 B A3.

Some sound modules use a protocol called General MIDI or GM. This is a system that allows arrangements played on different synthesizers to use the correct voices as long as they conform to GM. The voices are for all intents and purposes the same for all synthesizers: for example 067 means that synthesizer's version for Tenor Sax.

Dividing sequences

We are going to divide sequences. And we are going to use the scissors tool. The two are not always synonymous because one can divide sequences by using key commands, too. At any rate, get the scissors from the tool box and make it your working tool. You are still in the Arrange Screen, so we will first divide there.

Make a staff of 30 bars on an instrument on any channel. Place the scissors upon the track, say, at bar 7 and click. The staff is divided in two at bar 7. Click at bar 10. The staff is divided there. Rubber-band select the staff with its divided parts. The staff is blackened as it is selected. Choose the glue pot tool. Click anywhere on the staff. In an instant it is restored to wholeness. In a sense the glue pot is the opposite of the scissors.

Open the Score Screen. Do the same, that is, divide up the staff. You find that you are able to cut it down with the scissors. This is all the dividing you can do on the Score Screen. But you can do things a little easier on the Arrange Screen.

Go back to the Arrange Screen. Select the staff you have created. Place the SPL at a remaining measure using the square brackets. Press ⌃+Y. The staff divides at the SPL. Try a few cuts elsewhere. Remember to select the staff before you divide. You may want to restore the staff to wholeness along the way. The divide key commands are already programmed into the Mac. I see no reason to change them.

Here is a neat command to finish up our discussion of divide: the divide by locator command. Restore the staff to wholeness. Touch the select arrow to the upper part of the ruler and, while keeping it clicked, draw it to the right so that you have selected measure 4.1 to 10.1 (measure 4 beat 1.) A lightbar shows what you have selected. This by itself is called the cycle feature. It enables you to play the same measures over and over and work on them in other ways. If you were to press 'play', that same sequence would play endlessly. One way of dividing is to cut the staff at the locators (the end points of the cycle) by selecting cycle, selecting the staff and pressing ⌘+Y . You always know exactly where the locators are by looking at the first two addresses on the Transport Bar. Try dividing by locators a few more times.

Make sure the staff is restored to wholeness. Divide at the beginning of measures 9, 17, 25 and 33. You have the divisions of the AABA' structure: A1 consists of measures 1-8; A2, measures 9-16, B, the bridge 17-24; and A', measures 25-32. You now have created the four segments, A1, A2, B, and A'.

For selecting tools, such as the scissors tool or the glue pot, instead of moving the pointer to the instrument box, you can move the instrument box to the pointer wherever it may be by pressing [esc] . The entire toolbox will move to your mouse pointer. When you have chosen your tool, the toolbox disappears.

You can cut with the scissors or by using the SPL and a Key Command. Select the staff. Move the SPL along the staff to where you want it with the square bracket key, then cut it by pressing [Y] . I am having you cut with the method that uses the SPL so that you cut precisley on the first beat of the bar rather than free hand with the scissors alone. This command alone, if very near to the first beat will be 'rounded' to the nearest bar. Another way to get the SPL right on the bar is to center it with the [[] and []] , going first to the bar beyond, then back to where you really want to go.

The piece of the divided sequence to the right of the cut will be highlighted. Often you will want to delete the sequence to the right of the cut and that pre-selects it. Go to the Score Screen and look at what you have done. The point of all this is that you are going to copy a section many times and cutting the sequence precisely makes it easier to manipulate. There will be many exact cuts that you will be manipulating.

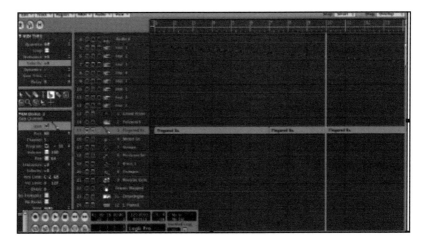

Dividing the Staff

The Undo Function

To see how Key Commands make life easier for us, let's start again at the point before we divided our 32 bar trumpet track. We use the undo function , ⌘+z to get back to an earlier point. Every press of ⌘+z undoes the most recent change to the program, stepping backwards. You can select how many undo step you can make (I have chosen 30) in >Logic >Preferences >Global >Editing. You can re-do, i.e. move forward from a ⌘+z action, by >Edit >Redo and clicking on 'Redo'.

Before you work on your song

Allow me to remind you that if you work yourself into a corner and want to go back to the last save, there is a menu choice (that you can make a Key Command) for reverting to the last save. It is found in menu File > Revert to Saved.

If you want to go back radically, load yesterday's saved version of the song. The program automatically saves a song as a Logic song with the suffix .lso. A good idea is to create a directory on another drive to save your daily, dated Logic work to. You may have a directory called Logic and two subdirectories: songs and audio files. And a third subdirectory for work in progress: temp. Since there are now inexpensive USB and Firewire external hard drives, you can back up to them as you go along. Do not forget about Cds - they are the cheapest, quickest backup medium around.

More Copying

A tip here: for accompaniment don't make a dull canvas of whole notes or half notes on beat with regular chord changes. I make it more interesting by first entering an easy (dull) pattern like whole note chords, then perking it up by creating a rhythmic pattern: for example, dotted quarter, eighth, eighth and dotted quarter. The rest is done with copying and note correction.

Dull Accompaniment

Lively Accompaniment

This is one reason why this book places such emphasis on copying. You are not opting out by using the same notes played by the same instrument or other instruments. The art of arranging lies in the ordering of effects, created by choice of instruments, accompaniments, rhythms and countermelodies. Enjoy your copying. It is the one mechanical activity that you will engage in. Examine a few arrangements and note the amount of copying. You will be surprised.

The more you know what you are copying the more you will enjoy it. That is why we have talked about melody lines, acompaniment, backgrounds, walking bass, song structure, choruses, guide tones, etc.

The first chorus of this arrangement has a simple spread ('pad') accompanying the melody. As mentioned, the melody is given to the bandoneon. Whenever you hear the bandoneon, think, 'this is really being perfomed by a live singer.' The second chorus has a solo trumpet acccompanied by the same spread. The bridge is given to clarinets, in order to introduce variety and to give the players a rest (although in real life the same players would be doubling on reed instruments. But we will pretend that we have an unlimited budget and that we can hire as many musicians as we want). In the same way we used 5 tenors in our arrangement of 'Drive Me Crazy' instead of the usual saxophone section.

Structurally we have made the song shorter by not having a second bridge. Instead, the song is made longer by the taglines given to the singer. The tag chorus consists of the same notes thoughout (with a few slight changes) which simplifies the arrrangement considerably.

Once you have made a first chorus, you can make an arrangement of sequences and the repetitions – indeed whole choruses – quickly on the Arrange Page using repetitions of notes played by the same or other instruments. It is important that the segments be labeled or that you remember what they are. Especially useful here is the copy command Alt plus mouse drag. You can create another chorus in the Arrange Screen by manipulating whole sequences. For example, in the first chorus of 'Flying and Feeling So Fine' you have the melody given to bandoneon and the accompaniment, a spread, given to the tenor saxes and the trombone. As an experiment, give the melody for a second chorus to the trumpet and the same spread to the tenor saxes and trombone. On the Arrange Screen drag copy the melody to trumpet 1, trombone to trombone, tenors 1 and 2 to tenors 1 and 2. drag-copy the bass, piano and drums, one by one to place in the second chorus. When you have finished play both choruses. You have made this chorus entirely in Arrange.

Instrument Sets

You have already been introduced to two important Logic functions: the Instrument Set and the Score Styles. A review and stepping through of these functions is in order. Let's take it from the very beginning. You have designated your basic group of instruments. For this group it is a medium combo. You will be spending a lot of time arranging for three winds. [please note: I use the terms 'winds, 'horns' and 'brass' to refer to the blown instruments.] You do not want to have extra staves like drums and contrabass cluttering up every screen you work on, just the three staves of the horns would be nice. At the top left of your Score Screen you have the group designated that you are working with. You have only one group, 'All Instruments', that you have been working with, so you have not noticed it.

We will create a group of the three horns you are working with so that you may comfortably call up only the three horns. When you are at the part of the arrangement where you want to work with all of the instruments at once, you can go back to the Instrument Set 'All Instruments' again.

One asumes that you are working in Score from which Instrument Set and Score Styles are accessed. Double-click on the 'All Instruments' rectangle. This opens the Instrument Set Window. Since you are making a new instrument set, click on the selection marked 'New'. You are faced with a number of options. You will learn to handle them in time, but for this example pick 'New Empty Set', then 'Add Instrument Entry'. Your instrument choices in the Environment will appear in the Instrument Set window; you can leave, delete, or change them later. After you have entered any three instruments with 'New', place the pointer on the existing first instrument, and holding the pointer down, choose the instrument you wish. Do the same with the other two instruments. Use the text pointer and change the name of the Instrument Set to something descriptive like '3 Horns'. Choose '3 Horns' in the Instrument Set window and there you have it – three staves. Create the Key Command Alt + N 'name instruments' in order to to see which instrument is which (they will appear on screen in the same order as in the Instrument Set Window. [Note: the new instruments have to exist already in the Environment Windows in order to be inserted in Instrument Sets.]

This is especially helpful when working on one section. There are numerous examples of the full sax section in this book. They were created with a separate sax Instrument Set. For practise, create an Instrument Set for a trumpet section. Remember to first create the instruments in Environment (MIDI). You will want to take the time to set up templates for combos, big band or orchestra – depending what instruments you work with – with section Instrument Sets.

While you are working you can make ad hoc Instrument Sets that will be helpful for a time, but that you do not have to keep. For example, if you want to add the bass, and the melody is in the alto sax, you can create an Instrument Set of just the bass and a lead instrument, place the bass line, and then delete the Instrument Set.

Also, you will be using this device so frequently you should use the Key Command you created for it ⌘ + ctrl + I   Incidentally, Logic gives you convenient ways to group the instruments in the Instrument Set window and in the Score. There are brackets, bars and barlines on the Instument Set Screen to isolate one section from another. How you set them in Instrument Set determines how they will appear in the Score. Remember that a staff only appears in the Score if it is put in the Instrument Set. The other instruments will play, but they will not have that written representation. You may want it so: to have several trumpets playing, but only one trumpet, the trumpet in the instrument set, showing up on the Score Screen.

Alternatively, you can write several parts but see and hear only one voice by muting those voices. Choose, in >File >Song Settings >Score >General to check the box 'Hide Muted Tracks' and mute those tracks in the Arrange Screen.

Score Style Window

The Score Style Window ⌘ + ctrl + S is somehow considered the corollary voice counterpart to the Instrument Set Window. It establishes, among other things, the type of clef that the instrument will use. For example, the clarinet is usually written in the treble clef but in a way that makes Bb represent the sound of C (doh). It is called Bb treble clef. The same is true for the soprano saxophone and the trumpet.

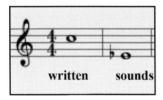

Alto Saxophone

Some instruments use tenor clef that is easier for the general trombone range. You do not have to use these clefs unless you are conversant with them. You can make clef changes at any time. That is why we encourage you to make these changes just before printing, and in a special file where you make these changes. A more easily understandable example is the case of the piano. The piano has two clefs, treble and bass, in concert pitch.

Laying out the plan - labeling

This method is not intended for working out the details of the arrangement - that will be done on paper. What is intended here is a road map to help you find your place on the screen while working. If you are going to copy the horns from A2 to position A3, you can find where A3 begins by the sequence labels on a track of empty bars. Create a track instrument in environment with 'new' and treat it like you would any MIDI instrument. Name it 'locate' and put it in the Arrange Screen. In Arrange, place it in order above the other instrument tracks by dragging on the number at the left side of the instrument name.

Our lead sheet tells us that IA1, IA2, IB, and IA3 (chorus one, first section A and so on) each have 8 bars. pencil-click to make bars and draw them out to 8 bars. Repeat the 8 bar sequence 3 times (R). Using the text tool, label the sequences A1, A1, B and A3. Group select the 32 bars and repeat it 3 times.

You can also keep track of your instruments, especially when you write for sections by making the saxophones one color, the trombones another. Some people make their verses one color and their choruses another. A very clever usage is to make all the trombone recordings red, and any edits of them in shades of red, so that they are still seen as being in the same family.

A Quick Way of Copying Parts

Here is a quick way of writing parts. We will write for a sax section. Make sure you have five staves with the appropriate saxophone assigned. Make a separate Instrument Set and instruments labeled 'sax section'. Choose this Instrument Set to get a clear picture of the saxes only. There are several ways of copying the sax parts:

Method 1

First create the melody. Select the melody and then use [alt] copy (dragging) to double the melody one octave down (this is the bari). You now only have three instruments to fill in. Use the Step Input Keyboard. You are going to place chords only on certain notes (not on all notes of the melody). Drag the SPL to where you want the chord. Set the appropriate note value. Play the three notes that are lacking in the five note chord. Repeat for the other notes.

You now have all five notes on one staff. Make sure that the section of staff you are working on is divided, i.e. cut off from the rest of the staff with one of the divide commands. In that section select the bottom line by using the

Key Command ⇧+↓ . The bottom line will then blink. Save this selected line with ⌘+c then transfer it to the baritone staff with ⌘+v . Be sure to have the SPL on the first bar first beat of the baritone staff. Go back to the original line, select the bottom line again (the baritone line) then delete it.

On the original staff, again select the bottom line. This is now the line for the second tenor saxophone (now that the baritone saxophone's line has been erased). After being selected the bottom line will blink. Transfer that line, then erase the original.

Continue doing that until all five lines are on their correct staves. (If you play the original chord on the alto sax staff you only have to move four lines). You can do everyting with ⇧+↓ . The command for selecting the top line is ⇧+↑ . Add these commands to your repertoire of key commands.

If you have not separated your work area (Logic refers to this as a 'region') on the staff by divisions created by one of the Y commands, the 'select bottom line' will act on the entire bottom line of the song, and when you go to delete the line...

Method 2.
Play all five notes in as a chord using the virtual keyboard. Then transfer them using ⇧+↓ .

Method 3.
Record it in live if you are a good keyboardist. Transfer the lines with ⇧+↓ .

Method 4.
Step in the parts using a MIDI keyboard and the step procedure followed by line by line transfer.

Method 5.
There is another method of part writing by using the demix and split to channel commands. This would only work of you used multiple channels in Score Styles. (See Chap. VI, Polphony). I find it unnecessarily complex and prefer the line by line method. I am mentioning this for the sake of completeness.

Another Way of Laying out the Plan - Markers

In addition to labelling the parts, you can mark events on the bar lines themselves. This is done with Logic's markers. Short texts appear on the bar ruler of the edit windows and longer texts appear upon examination of the markers or in the marker text window. In Arrange, click on the options menu and select 'marker' and then 'create'. A marker appears at the SPL. Click again on 'marker' and then 'quick edit' and a name field on the marker opens up. Play with the marker options. You see you can create markers wherever you want them and by opening up the text window, create texts of different lengths.

It is also handy to know where to go to when you have left an arrangement for several days. You open the list of markers and immediately can find the section you wish to work on.

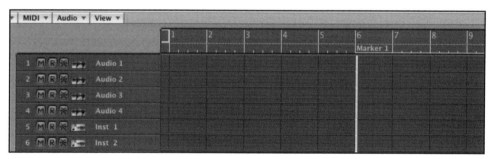

A Marker

You can automate the marker functions with Key Commands. Make the following assignments:

create marker	⌘ + alt + ↑
open marker list	⌘ + L
go to previous marker	⌘ + alt + ←
go to next marker	⌘ + alt + →
go to marker #	⌘ + alt + M
delete marker	⌘ + alt + ↓
open marker text	⌘ + T

This allows you to navigate through your arrangement by markers, going from section to section. Experiment with markers. You will find that learning about them is time well spent. When you are mixing you can open the Marker List window as a floating window under Options >Marker >Open List as Float. and move to the marker section you desire by clicking on it in the list.

Other ways to navigate through the arrangement – a review

Set a go to command as |G_| in Key Commands to help you get around. To go to a particular bar, make sure the bar is showing (by moving the position slider at the bottom of your page or Command scroll wheel), then click just under the ruler of the bar.

Or use the square bracket keys [[ ] [ ]] which have been assigned to 'advance' and 'rewind'. I sometimes use these commands for backing up and listening two or three times to a section rather than using the option of blocking out a section for cycle mode.

Playing Your Work

You will want to play your work through as you go along. You can play the whole song from the beginning or from any point in the song. The song plays from the location of the SPL if given the command from the Transport Bar. In Logic the Key Command for play is assigned to the space bar. If you are working on a group of bars – maybe a bridge – and will be listening to it a lot, select the measures in question on the ruler and turn the cycle function on with the Transport Bar. Then 'play'. The |0_| of the number pad set to 'stop' puts the SPL back to bar 1. It will be used frequently.

'Scrub' plays what the SPL is dragged over by the mouse when the pause button has been clicked on. I find this especialy useful for checking harmonies.

Checking a Small Section

Not available to Logic Express, there is a procedure for listening at any place in the score called the 'scrub' procedure. Find or create a chord to listen to. Locate the SPL near it. Turn on the scrub command of the Transport Bar [pause button], grab the SPL with the pointer click and hold the SPL, and drag it across the chord. If the MIDI Out on the score Screen is turned on, you should be able to hear the chord. You can scrub one chord or a whole song as long as you are holding and moving the SPL across the score. You can think of it as an out of tempo 'play' where you control the speed of the SPL. Scrub is especially useful when writing sectional harmony or tutti harmony (all sections playing at once). It makes it convenient to hear single chords and one chord moving into another.

Another Neat Way

A way to play a section of our song over and over is to create the Key Command 'set locators by objects'. Find this Key Command and assign `alt` + `0` to it. When you want to hear something, highlight the objects you wish to cycle around, and then press this command. Make sure 'cycle' is on. The SPL will automatically start at the first bar you want played and will continue moving until you stop the cycle-playing.

Makes Everything Easier

A device, actually a convention among musicians, that makes reading and writing easier, is that in times that have four beats, beat three is always shown. Doing so makes complex rhythms and off-beats easier and quicker to read. You do not have to show beat three in passages with notes of greater duration.

Showing Beat 3   Not Showing Beat 3

Copy the Song

Now you can begin copying 'Flying'. Prepare the instruments in the Environment and then in the Arrange Page. Copy the first chorus melody in the Score using any of the techniques mentioned. For practise, use a technnique that is unfamiliar to you. Create the second chorus from as many elements of the first chorus as you can, then in the same way the tag lines and accompaniments. Put in your expression and dynamic markings, save and close your song. Make your final ⌘+S , close the song and take a well-deserved break.

Chapter VI: Writing for More Voices

We are going to write for more voices, but before beginning, we should ask ourselves what we are trying to achieve by writing for a greater number of instruments. Some answers come to mind quickly: to write an arrangement that has a bigger and more interesting sound; to create a richer sound than with a small number of instruments; and to combine harmonies and melody at the same time. All true.

Good writing explains the harmony clearly and thus advances the song. Explaining means conveying clearly which chord is intended. The most important tones for conveying this are the third and the seventh of the chord (sometimes the sixth). Avoiding the third or seventh tone is a special technique and gives a vague, floating sound.

Good harmonic writing is smooth writing. Elements do not stick out and call attention to themselves. We are working toward a united, unified sound. This is not to say that different types of textures should not be used. An interchange of textures adds contrast and interest to your work. Good arranging is like good cooking. It should taste delicious, but none of the spices should predominate. You may be able to taste a little dill or nutmeg, a bit of basil or a dash of rosemary, but not to the detriment of the total recipe. The listener should enjoy the whole, not be distracted by its parts.

Let's run through a few three voice techniques that will help us write good arrangements. Do not forget that at any time you can replace basic scale tones (the notes 1, 3, 5, maj7) with tension tones (tones other than scale tones). For example:

Basics

Let's go over some basics of harmony writing, whether for three, four or more voices. Pay attention to the basic vocabulary. Remember that this is not a full course in arranging. It is an introduction to the vocabulary and techniques used in arranging. It takes several courses over many years to become a good arranger. Meanwhile, listen carefully to great arrangers like Sammy Nestico and Maria Schneider and experiment freely with Logic. Important words will be italicized in the text. Get in the habit of using them.

First of all, a chord is either *open* or *closed*. Closed *voicings* consist of the basic triad of the chord plus the sixth or the seventh tone. The illustration immediately shows that the notes of a closed chord are next to each other in order in the chord, e.g. C - A - G - E (from the top down) in a C6 chord, with no omissions of notes. Or in the G7 chord with a B lead (melody) B - G - F - D. Open refers to a wider distribution of notes with an omission or omissions, and this kind of chord is therefore spread out over a wider area. Distribution of notes (chord tones) are also referred to as voicings. Some closed voicings are shown for the basic chord types:

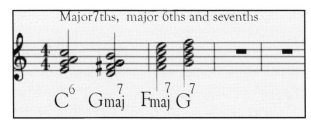

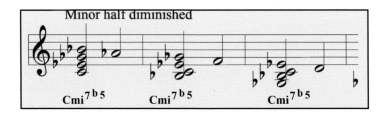

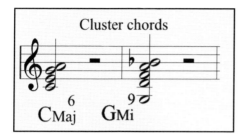

Chord types are used depending on the melodic range in which they appear. Closed voicings consist of a triad plus a 6th or a 7th. They have a compact sound. They appear when the melody note is from middle C to C an octave above middle C and the melody is not repeated in a higher register.

Sometimes the term 'cluster' is used when discussing closed chords. A Chord is a 'cluster chord' or is said to 'contain a cluster' when two of its notes are touching (minor or major seconds). Clusters are sequential, where notes of the

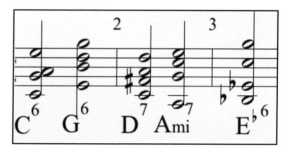

triad are not skipped, or non-sequential, where a note or notes of the triad is skipped. It is always a tension note plus a triadic note that forms the cluster. For example, chords built on triads plus major sixth or seventh are cluster chords. Clusters can also be formed by replacement tones, for example minor V chords with the ninth added forms a cluster between the second (ninth) A and minor third Bb.

A way of classifying clusters is calling them 'cluster 3rd below' or 'cluster fourth below'. Hopefully the examples make further description unnecessary. This type of chord often appears just under a treble melody. Sometimes the third and fourth clusters are mixed. Very atmospheric.

Another important term is *range* of the voicing. There is some overlap, but generally the height of the pitch of the melody note determines whether the voicing is closed or open. The range of open chords is from F above middle C to the F an octave higher. There is an overlap where either chord type can be used.

Omitting a Voice

One method of writing for three voices is to write for four voices and omit one of the four. This means the fourth (bottom), third, or second voice. You do this either when you only have three instruments or are striving for the effect this kind of writing gives.

Chord Species

The type of chord formed, based on how it is constructed, is called the *species* of the chord. At this point, we will show the various species of four voice chords. Keep in mind that these chords are built on their triads plus six or seven, plus there is the possibility of replacing tones.

Drop-2

When the melody note is above C or D above the staff, a common voicing called '*drop two*' is employed. This means that the second voice of a normal closed voicing is moved to the bottom of the chord. In the range shown here you often find drop 2 chords occurring.

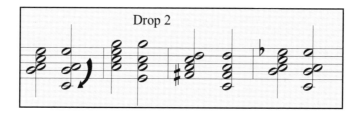

In the same range shown above for drop two you can also drop the third note of the closed chord making a '*drop-3*'. [The first chord shows the underlying structure and is not played.]

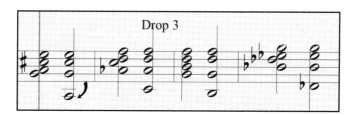

In the upper range of drop 2 and drop 3 shown below, you can employ a technique called '*drop-2+4*'. [The first chord shows the underlying structure and is not played.]

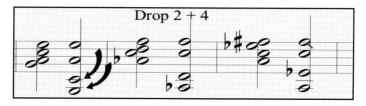

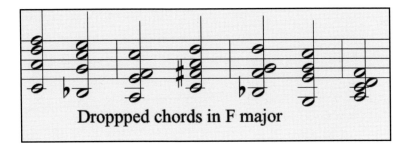

Droppped chords in F major

All species of chords. Identify the chords as Drop-2, Drop-3 etc.

Importance of the key

We have seen that certain voicings are chosen according to the pitch of the melody note. If you have a dropped voicing, which should occur an octave above middle C, in the wrong range, i.e. below that C, they do not sound good. For that reason you can not take an arrangement made in the key of F and transpose it directly to a key 5 or 6 tones away. It is easy to transpose in Logic: just select all the notes and move them down or up and change a few sharps or flats. But you must be careful.   Experiment with it yourself. There are *acoustic laws* which always prevail. Acoustically something either sounds good or bad.   There is no middle ground.   You cannot improve something if it is flawed acoustically.   For example, a chord in the wrong range will always sound poorly, no matter which instruments play it nor how softly or loudly it is played.

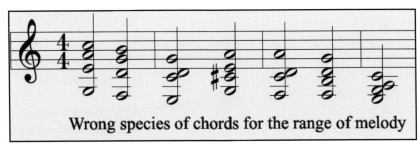

Wrong species of chords for the range of melody

Minor second intervals

Minor second intervals (also called semitone intervals) are treated with special care. In many chords they can sound close and wonderful, minor sevenths for example, when directly below a chord tone. When a minor second is created across the interval of an octave, a minor ninth is created. This minor 9 interval should be avoided. We perceive it as 'ugly' and it sticks out. You can avoid this by changing a major seventh to a sixth as shown.

Also, you should avoid using the minor second interval in any range between the top two voices, either by using a drop voicing or change the major 7th to a major 6th. The interval of a second is too close to be used by the two top voices.

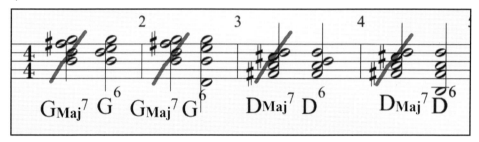

Other important concepts

Doubling

A frequently used device of big band arranging is the sectional solo of the saxophone section. When the entire section plays, the baritone sax commonly *doubles* the melody but an octave lower. The baritone sax plays the same melody an octave lower than the lead sax. If dropped voicings place a bass note lower than the melody, this note is played by another tenor sax. The baritone continues playing the melody. The impression given is of the melody doubled, and it does not matter if a lower chord note or notes appears, played by a different sax. There is enough continuity of the melody provided by the doubling.

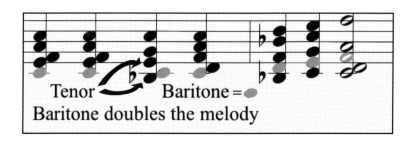

Baritone doubles the melody

In normal playing, the same instrument does not play the same note twice in a row. In places where the same note sounds twice, one instrument interchanges the note with a neighboring (same) instrument, creating a line in which he plays the note once and his neighbor plays the note once. This is true of two trumpets, two trombones, two saxes, etc. But if the tempo is quite slow the same instrument may play the same note twice.

Limits of low intervals

Another acoustic truth that must be observed has to do with the *lower limits* of intervals. Play the following chords on your piano or synth using the trombone or bassoon voice Hear how muddy and unclear they sound.

Obviously then, there are acoustic limits to the closeness of tones in the lower range. Be guided by your hearing for acceptable low limits. Experiment a bit at the keyboard. Normally E3 or Eb3 is considered the limit for seconds, C3 the limit for minor thirds, Bb3 the limit for major thirds or fourths and bigger intervals are allowed down to tenths with Bb2.

Some techniques for Three Voice Writing

You do not have to include the *root (fundamental)* of the chord in your three voices. The bass conveys that part of the explanation of the harmony. The desire to feel the fundamental of a chord is so strong in us that even when it is not there we somehow intuit it.

Here is a list of possible ways to handle three voices. The discussion may seem overly mechanical, but keep in mind that using a method, even for a few bars or a chorus provides the important quality of consistency to your music. Of course the range of the melody will dictate some chord type choices. And you may mix some chord types. Let your ear be your guide.

1) Unison

Creates a big sound. The simplest way is to have passages in unison. This conveys the melody with a bang and, with a good rhythm section providing harmony, can be very effective. The piano or guitar along with the bass provides the harmony, the instruments sound particularly powerful. Of course, this is not to be used too much.

2) Unison interspersed with harmony

Especially effective for some kinds of writing are short passages in unison that end in three voice harmony.

3) Guide tones. *'Spread'*.

Guide tones refer to tones three and six or seven. When guide tones or their substitutes plus the fundamentals are used as 'pads' below melodies they constitute a style of arranging known as *'spread'*. This is a technique of accompaniment that is based on having (at least) the fundamental (chord tone) and the guide tones in the cello range supporting the melody.

There is limited movement in each part, and the bass rarely goes lower than F2 (it can be doubled). Often arrangers speak of providing *pads* under a singer. This is 'spread'. Spread can be done by bass and baritone sax or bass and two tenor saxes, or three trombones. Depending on the style of music, other instruments can be used. You will recognize this sound instantly as it is used so frequently.

The lowest voice plays the fundamental. Voices 2 and 3 play the guide tones, voice one plays the melody.

4) Sixth below

Add the sixth or seventh below the melody note then add a guide tone between that and the melody. Add the fundamental in the fourth voice. The result of this method is very similar to spread. Sometimes there is no room to put the guide tone or you find that that you must respect the lower limit rules. If necessary exchange voices so that the guide tone fits.

5) Melody plus dissonant cluster.

As mentioned, a cluster is a chord in which two notes (or more) touch. Some clusters are made by adding the seventh, major or minor, to its triad. Or substituting tone 4 for 5. A cluster can also be created by substituting tone 3 for tone 2. Alternatively you can describe this process as clustering a tone with a tension tone and skipping a triad tone.

6) Drop 2

You already know that this is a way of producing a more open sound by opening up a chord based on the triad. You skip the second note from the top and transfer it to the bottom of the chord. You can also form drop 2 on the basis of a cluster.

7) Third plus an octave

Harmonizing a third, major or minor, from the melody and adding an octave below. This is a refreshing sound when used sparingly.

Combining sections

The presentation of chord species deals with combining groups of different *sections*, or groups of the same instruments, such as the 'sax section' or the 'trumpet section'. Very often the sections are combined so that you get a blast of brass with the trumpets together with the trombones, a full *tutti* sound of all three sections playing together. The saxophone section covers such a wide range of sound it is often given a whole A or B all to itself. The sections can combine in different ways: the trumpets, irrespective of how high they are, play a triad and repeat the top note, the trombones can double them (without skipping) or can play a cluster of four notes under them. The saxes can either play notes of the chord, doubling some of the notes played by the trombones, or they can play spread. The trombones can either play or not, sometimes doubling the trumpets, sometimes playing spread.

If the melodic movement of the section or sections combined is very jagged or irregular it is said to be *dynamic*. The best kind of *deployment* of the sections is to have the trumpets playing closed (despite the height of the melody) and the trombone or saxes directly under the trumpets, also played closed. Alternatively, you can use a dynamic melodic deployment: the top section playing closed but the bottom section using spread. This is usually the form of the last tutti chorus of a big band arrangement. When you examine other arrangements, try to differentiate between the different strategies of deployment.

The many arranging possibilities may be making your head swim. A lot of your decisions will require judgement. You will develop judgement and mature as as you arrange and listen carefully to other arrangers.

These tips on arranging round out this section. Three voice chords that are spread across too wide a range sound empty, and they should be altered. An open fifth tone sticks out, so it should not be used. Listen to the effect a passage with a particular chord species has. Does it sound good? Is it what you want? Does it sound balanced? This is what you should constantly ask yourself.

As a rule, if the melody is angular (moves jaggedly and largely), the accompaniment is *static* and balancing. Or conversely, if the melody is static, the accompaniment can be full of movement and angularity.

Chapter VII: Printing

You have previously seen a printed lead sheet. It was adequate for your singer and pianist and was even good enough to give to a record producer. You are going to learn to print scores and parts, and to adjust the pages to print well. You will learn to check final touches and to prepare the score for printing. You will print parts where each player gets his own individual part and the director gets a full score.

Photocopy your saved version of 'Hotcha!' in Appendix II. This is a version for printing, and not for playing a recording; we have no doubled tracks or extra instruments for enriching the sound. You see multiple instruments playing identical parts in the printed version of 'Hotcha!'.

In the mix version of all the songs (on the CD) the attacks of the brass instruments were doubled and made staccato to give the instrument extra life. The same is true of delaying the 'other' trumpet, which was also added for richness. We do not wish to show these tracks in the print version. Sound is not important in this version, only the look. In the print version, I deleted those tracks. One could have muted all the redundant tracks and checked the 'Hide Muted Tracks' in the General Screen, to be discussed shortly. I chose to eliminate these tracks. Only one track is shown for each instrument. In the 'mix' version empty staves are eliminated for showing up entrances and flourishes and solos and other parts of the score.

Make sure we are using an appropriate font. If you were doing a page from the 'Real Book' or a jazz lead sheet you could consider using the Jazz Font, which is available, as are others, at www.jazzfont.com.

There are other fonts available for specific uses. You might someday consider buying other fonts, but the font that comes with the program, Sonata, is fine for general usage. To add fonts, copy the desired font to your Logic directory. Open the menu Logic > Preferences > Score. Once there, choose the font in the font box. If you have the program font installed, the box will not accept a response unless 'Use External Font' is checked. If you now open the score window you will notice that the font is the new font, Jazz. You will recognize it immediately. The font will remain unchanged if there has been a mistake in the loading or placement of a new font.

Move the SPL to the beginning of the song.

Using the 'drag-scroll' or 'measure-by-measure' movement of the SPL, one checks the alignment of the lyrics and chords and adjusts them if necessary. Now the arrangement is read again for quantization, slurring, beams, accidentals, note values and pitches. You make your corrections as you go along. Save after each correction. Proofread further, making sure that the clefs and key signatures are correct.

'Aliases' are carbon copies of a working phrase. Changes made to the working track are automatically made in the alias as well. You create an alias by holding down ⬆+alt when dragging the original. The use of aliases can be very handy in certain songs where you are still writing the melody or where the melody is repetitive. I rarely use them, because I consider them be an additional, unwanted complexity. If any aliases are present, this is the time to convert them to normal tracks with Arrange Screen >Midi >Alias >Turn to Real Copy (the alias to be converted must be selected).

On the Arrange Screen make sure that the sequences are glued together or are butted up against each other. This 'connects up' the sequences from start to finish. This 'connecting' is the opposite of 'clean-up' before mixing, where one eliminates the blank passages. I glued the segments together, by rubber band selecting the segments or by selecting the track (and hence all the segments within the track) and then using the glue tool. I could also have 'butted' the sequences next to each other by extending them using the lower right or left hand corner. It does not matter in printing scores; things will print.

the same whether butted or glued, except for the clef. In printing parts, unless you connect the segments with the glue tool, you will print only the segment selected and not the whole part.

Connecting Sequences

Go to the Score Screen and page mode 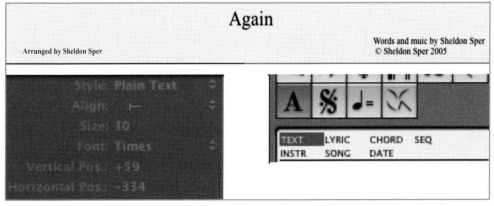 If the score does not designate the title, composer, arranger and copyright notice and date, do so now. In the Score Screen, select the text symbol from the part box. The lower parameter box asks you which font and size you want. The title of the song goes on the on the 'header' of the print copy. This means the heading part of page 1. Adjust the title to the type and size desired in the parameter box. Identify who wrote the music and words, if any, and, importantly, 'arranged by' and the appropriate copyright notices. Adjust them, if necessary. Make the appropriate font, size and margin formatting adjustments in the parameter box of the score screen. The right and left placement of chords is made in the 'Horizontal Pos.' choice in the parameter box. You already know how to align vertically from doing it to lyrics and chords.

Header

Adjusting Margins by Dragging or Using General Screen

Make side margin adjustments either in the >File >Song Setting >Score >General screen or by dragging on them in the Score Screen (first, you have to enable 'print view' in order to see the page margins) or by dragging on them In Score window local menu, View >Print View.

Adjusting Margins

Users of versions other than Logic 7 will find the settings in the Song Setting menus for margins, page and bar numbers etc. Look in Arrange >File >Song Settings Score >General on the Arrange Screen.

[Note: The settings windows in the different versions are similar. The settings for Logic Pro 7 and Logic Pro 6 are shown. For example, in Logic 7, you have the choices indicated by icon and word. Examine them. A lot of the settings are self-evident. Experimenting with the settings is the quickest way to learn. Print out your changes; somehow the errors are more evident in printout form than on the screen. You can print a few pages; you do not have to print the whole score].

We will examine the General Screen in detail. This page starts out with the margin settings. You have already seen them. They refer to the printable area of the printer page. For example, your printer may create a top margin of 1 cm. The margin set by you will then be in addition to the margin set by your printer. You can also adjust the right and left margins of individual staves by clicking near the edge of the staff and dragging or pushing with the layout tool .

'Add Bracket Space' creates more space for brackets in addition to the left margin that you have designated. If you do not check this option the left margin will be set to the limit that you have indicated.

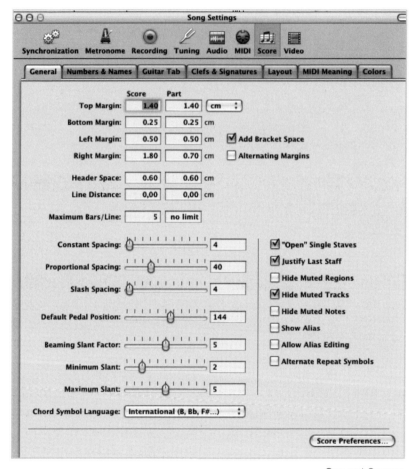

General Screen

'Alternating Margins' sets the margins as in a book with facing pages, where the right margin of the right hand page is equal to the left margin of the left hand page. 'Header Space' refers to the area where you put your title, copyright and credits. It applies to the first page only. This does not matter if you are printing parts, but, when printing a score, the header and all of the staves of the score have to fit on page one. Then the bars alone will fit on the subsequent pages.

Maximum Bars per Line' limits the number of bars per line. You can create easy-to-read lead sheets with only four bars per line. You also use this to give a more spacious look to the printout. You can override this setting on a line- by-line basis by dragging with the layout tool.

'Constant and Proportional Spacing' controls the horizontal distance between notes. Constant spacing refers to the distance between notes regardless of note value in relation to laying the notes out. 'Proportional spacing' takes the note value into account in spaces with longer spaces for half notes and shorter spaces for eighth notes. You will notice that two quarter notes take up roughly the space of one half note. Usually setting both controls will give best results.

Constant Spacing

Proportional Spacing

Now is a good time to 'clean up' chords that have moved to the wrong place. Use the sliders or telescope at top right of your Score Screen. If you have an older version with telescopes, click on the small end of the telescope to reduce the page in page view. This is not a print setting, but it is good for finding misplaced chords or lyrics. The best way to see the fit is to Later, you will be shown other methods for affecting the distance between lines and hence score size. You can experiment with all of these means.

'Slash Spacing' refers to the spaces between slashes. Slashes are often used in drum and bass parts to indicate beats. If you alternate slashes with bars containing notes, you should experiment with this setting to achieve a balanced look.

'Default Pedal Position' refers to the vertical placement in relation to the instrument's staff of the pedal symbol. You can also place this symbol manually with the mouse.

'Beaming Slant Factor' determines the angle of slant of the beams. Generally, higher numbers increases the slant. Experiment and set them to taste.

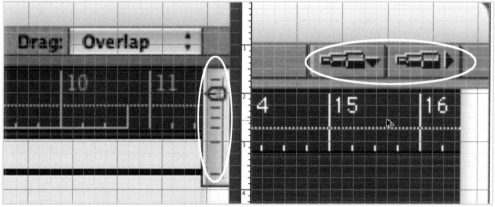

Screen Scaling (Not Permanent)

'Chord Symbol Language' depends on what kind of music and where you are writing. You can choose among International (includes American style) or German style.

'Justify Last Staff' lengthens the last bar to a full staff position.

'Hide Muted Regions-Tracks-Notes' (three boxes) keeps muted objects from being displayed. This is important when printing a score which uses the multiple instrument techniques discussed in the next chapters. actually print one page of your score. You can then adjust clef size or the distance between staves as you will do shortly. The idea is to make Logic's page fit the printer's page. I will say this again when we get to printing.

'Show Alias' is self explanatory.

'Allow Alias Editing' is also self explanatory.

'Alternate Repeat Symbols' displays your repeat signs with directional brackets. [label directional brackets]

Alternate Repeat Symbols

Score Clefs and Signatures

Choose another icon or tab in the Song Settings option, that of Score Clefs and Signatures. You may choose from the clef's pull down menu how and where to display the clefs. You can display them only on the first page or on every page. If you insert a change of clef from the part box, you can designate if that clef should appear smaller. 'Display Warnings at Line Breaks', shows 'warning' clefs, time signatures or key signatures at the end of a stave system when the change is at the beginning of the next measure.

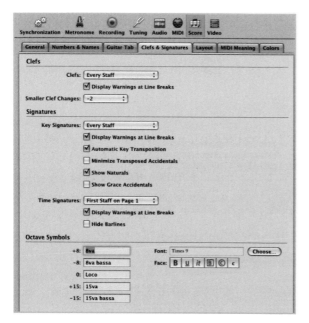

As always, the comfort of the musicians should be the most important criterion. For live players I put the clefs and signature on every page. If a synthesizer plays strings or other instruments I just put the clefs on every page.

Clef Adjustment Page

Score Numbers & Names

Switch to 'Numbers & Names'. You might not want page numbers, since the bar numbers already do the job of indicating the page order. 'Page offset' indicates on which page you wish to start. If you do not want to number the first two pages which only indicate the title and instruments used, you indicate a page offset of 2. Pages 3, 4, 5 etc. will then be numbered 1, 2 ,3.

You can number every bar or every fourth bar or every sixth bar. You choose the frequency of numbering with the step function. Bar offset is the number that is added to the actual bar number that is displayed. If you want the third bar to be labelled 'bar 1' you indicate an offset of three and a start of one.

You may choose to display the bar numbers at the bar line or at bar centre with the Horizontal Position box.

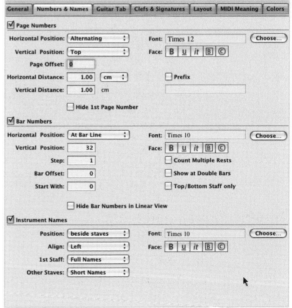

Names and Numbers

'Hide Numbers in Linear View' hides the measure numbers in the program where they are usually shown. Linear View refers to non-Page View, sometimes called 'scroll view' (when the page view button is deselected). It does not affect the print display.

'Instrument names' is pretty self-evident. You have the option of displaying the long name on the first page of the print-out and a short name on subsequent pages. You usually adjust this when you have occasion to use the Instrument Set Box.

Score Layout Parameters

Logic 6 and earlier versions call these 'extended layout parameters', Logic 7 simply calls them 'Layout'. Here you define settings for line thickness, the stem length, the distance between dots and their notes. These are settings too fine to deal with here. I can only advise you to experiment with these settings and change them to your taste as you acquire experience with the program.

Layout

Printing Scores and Parts

I have included examples of print-outs in this section. Originally I wanted the reader to load a basic song, make changes to it, then see the printed results. As noted, earlier versions of Logic will not load a later Logic's songs. I use Logic 7, so only that or later versions of Logic will load my songs. Not to mention the problem with Windows' versions. But the principles remain the same, so if you read along, you will master printing with Logic.

If you have many segments on the Arrange Screen, even if they are 'butted up' you will only get a score (notated) version of that segment. They must be glued to give you a view of the whole single part or to print a single part. Or you can double-click on the grey area of the Score Screen to view all of the segments of all of the parts.

After glueing all of the segments choose a single part. Or you can see a full page of that part in either scroll or page mode.Now choose page mode by clicking on the same scroll mode button. You see a full page of that single part. If you double-click in page mode you go directly to the part screen.

First edit the part as to margins and line spacing, especially if the part is long and needs many pages. Make sure that the chord symbols are placed correctly; if not,click and drag them where they belong. In Score you select a staff then Layout >Score Styles or you can adjust the clef size and the closeness of that staff to the next staff above and below it. Experiment with 6 as a clef size and 50 as a closeness setting. The images of the space settings should clarify this.

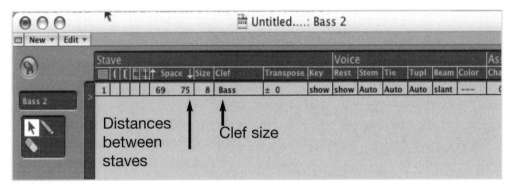

As formerly stated, the idea basic to printing in Logic is to make Logic's page fit your printer's page. You make the elements on Logic's page smaller, so that they fit on Logic's printer page. You do this by scaling down, reducing the space between clefs or reducing the clef sizes themselves or a combination of all these methods.

Close 'Hotcha!' 'BBGM' (Big Band General MIDI) is a good song for testing. Follow my creation of 'BBGM'. It is a big band set-up with 19 staves: 5 reeds, 4 trumpets, 4 trombones, piano (2 staves), bass and drums. I have placed piano staves for bass and drum to increase the number of staves to experiment with. I have also put notes in the Tenor 2 part so that the width will remain unaffected. There are enough staves to exceed a single normal page (I say 'overlap the page'). I have included a screenshot of the Arrange Screen and the Environment Screen for your convenience. You might find it helpful to create a 'BBGM' template with me.

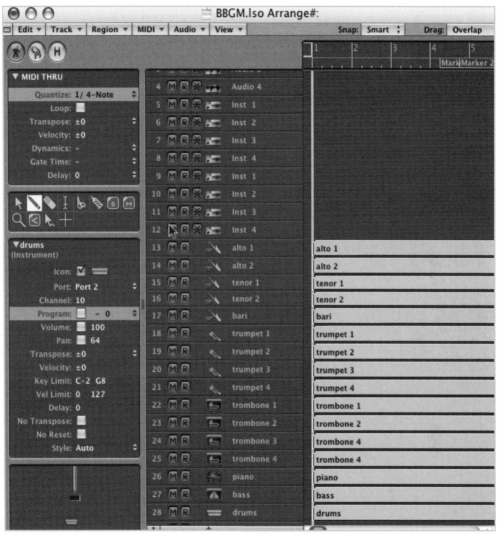

BBGM

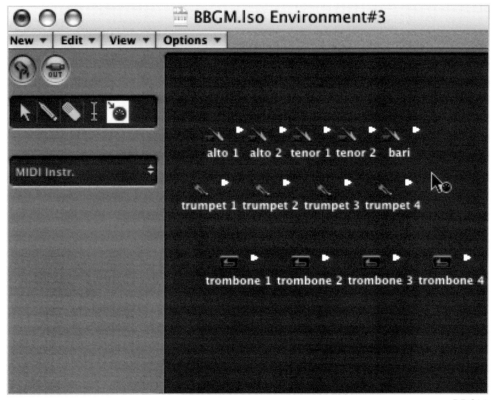

BBGM

A helpful exercise in coming to a printing decision is to put a summary of the print job at the bottom of each page. For example, at the bottom of this page I would put the clef size, line distance and scale in this way:

Staves=11/19   Cl=8   Ldist. Above=70   Below=70   Lscale=100
Pscale=100

'Lscale' refers to the scale set in Logic with any Instrument Set except 'All Instruments'; 'Pscale' is printer scale, set with the printer.

This means that I have set the space between staves above and below to 70, the clef size of all clefs used (treble and bass) to 8, and that the scale of Instrument Set is left at the default values of 100 per cent. The page does not fit the score; only 11 out of 19 staves fit on the page.

The page follows.

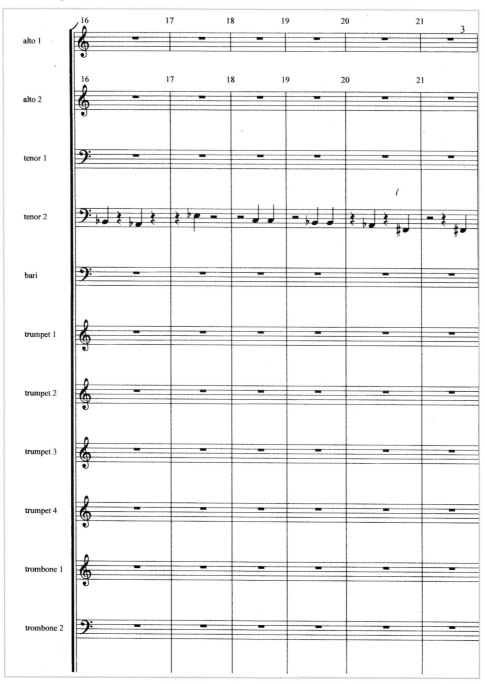

Staves=11/19   Cl=8   Ldist. Above=70 Below=70   Lscale=100
Pscale=100   Unsatisfactory   Image 1 Page from BBGM

We'll get to printing shortly, but first let's talk about viewing your Logic pages or should I say previewing. In page mode, let us get familiar with 'Print View'. This is turned on from >View in >Score.

We already know that this view is for adjusting the margin settings. It also gives one a horizontal view of all of the pages one is about to print if the scale slider on the right side is set very small. It allows you to count how many pages you are going to print. The printer also tells you how many pages will be printed at that setting, which is a clue to your settings.

Pages: ○ All	
◉ From: 1	to: 9

(?) (Preview) (Save As PDF...) (Fax...)   (Cancel) (Print)

Printer Count

Turn 'Print View' off. The page view is horizontal. Set the scale at the side of the page to very small with the slider or the telescopes, depending on which version of Logic you have. You also get a view of how many pages will be printed. I have found these settings unreliable for showing overlap from page to page and recommend them only for gross estimation. Look at these images.

The third viewing alternative is that provided by your own printer in collaboration with Mac's preview program. In Logic using ⌘+p will take you to page setup in advance of actual printing. At this point you verify that all the image appears within your chosen paper size and can then proceed to print.

Remember, we are printing a big band score.

We know from our first printing that these settings are too large. Printing without adjustment, i.e. with clef size 8 and scale = 100 percent and with the stave distance set to 70 above the staff and 70 below truncates your staves, printing only part of the band, not the whole band. The whole of Logic's page does not fit on the printer page so it is not satisfactory. Make a summary like the following to help you come to a printing decision. The score does not fit the printed page so these settings are unsatisfactory. Let us try a clef size of 6, line distance of 70.

Staves=13/19   Clef=6   Ldist Above=70 Below=70 Lscale 100   Pscale 100 Unsatisfactory. See image 2 on following page. (All print related images can be identified by the fraction of printed staves to the total number of staves in the summary.)

I make the elements on Logic's page a little smaller by reducing the distance between clefs from 70 to 50 (the piano clefs were set to 50 above and 60 below so I leave the piano alone) and I keep the size of the clefs at 6. You can adjust the first stave to the header by renaming the first stave under the header 'treble 1' or 'sol' or something similar and by adjusting the vertical distance above to 70 or 100 and using it only on page 1 of your score. You can use 'treble' with other staves on further pages.

Staves=15/19   Clef=6   Ldist Above=50 Below=50 Lscale 100   Pscale 100
Also unsatisfactory. (See image 3.)

The score is still too big for the page so I will adjust the clef size down to size 5 and keep the width between staves set to 50. The effect of the scale setting of the printer or of the score   is the same. Choose one or the other. There are still too many staves, which is unsatisfactory. It shows part of the staves, only 14 of them.

Staves=16/19   Clef=5   Ldist Above=50 Below=50 Lscale 100   Pscale 100
Also unsatisfactory. (See image 4.)

Staves=13/19 Clef=6   Ldist Above=70 below=70 Lscale 100
Pscale 100. Unsatisfactory.

Image 2 - Page from BBGM

Staves=15/19   Clef=6   Ldist Above=50 below=50 Lscale 100
Pscale 100. Unsatisfactory.

Image 3- Page from BBGM

Staves=16/19 Clef=5   Ldist Above=50 Below=50 Lscale 100
Pscale 100. Unsatisfactory.

Image 4- Page from BBGM

I keep the line distance to 50 and the clef size to 5.
Staves=18/19 Clef=4 Ldist Above=50 Below=50 Lscale 100 Pscale 100
Also unsatisfactory. (See image 5.)

We are getting close. I try a line distance of 50, above and below, and a clef size of 5. Before that gave us 16/19. So I reduce the scale in Logic with Instrument Set by 20% to 80% or in the printer scale. I can reduce the scale in Logic using instument set or I can use the scale of the printer. I choose to use Logic's scale. That gives us a nice page where everything fits.
Staves=19/19 Clef=5   Ldist Above=50 Below=50   Lscale 80   Pscale 100
Satisfactory. (See image 6.)

Clef size 4 also nearly worked. I will try that at a reduction of l0% to 90%. Those settings also produce a workable page. So I have two settings to choose between that work. You see how this is a trial and error process.
Staves=19/19   Clef=4   Ldist Above=50 Below=50 Lscale 90   Pscale 100
Satisfactory. (See image 7.)

After getting the knack of printing score sheets, printing parts is easy. Selecting a track on the Arrange Screen and then going to the Score Screen will produce a preview screen and print screen of only that single part. The Score Screen shows only the selected part until you double-click the background of the screen. (Or you can use   and choose 'part' instead of 'score', if you have set up your own instrument sets.) When printing parts you can scale a part or reduce the size of the clefs, but you probably will not have to in order to produce legible, good looking parts.

A clever way of finding page fit is to preview or print out an end page of your score. If your printer tells you that your score is 31 pages, preview or print out page 30 in case the final page is short.

Staves=18/19 Clef=4 Ldist Above=50 Below=50 Lscale 100
Pscale 100. Unsatisfactory.

Image 5 - Page from BBGM

Staves=19/19 Clef=5 Ldist Above=50 Below=50 Lscale 80
Pscale 100. Satisfactory

Image 6- Page from BBGM

Staves=19/19 Clef=4 Ldist Above=50 Below=50 Lscale 90
Pscale 100. Satisfactory.

Image 7 - Page from BBGM

Printing lead sheets

If you have too many staves for one page, your first step should be pulling the first stave down at the first clef. That forces the staves further along on two pages and allows you to regulate the distance. Here are versions of 'Again' where the spacing of the lines has been changed by pulling the first clef of the first measure downwards. One illustration shows all of the lines, the entire song, on one page. The others show the song on two and three pages. This ability to regulate is especially useful if you are printing a single part or a leadsheet.

Regulating the page

Polyphonous Staves

An interesting and useful digression is to discuss writing polyphonically.

If you are writing passages for two instruments or more that are not soli, you will want to write different rhythms for each instrument, but on the same staff. You can only write them using a polyphonous staff style. Polyphonous refers to many voices and means that the voices may act independently from each other (as to time and pitch).

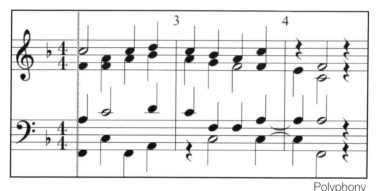

Polyphony

Among your staff styles are styles for piano and organ saying 1/2+3/4. This means two clefs and four separate parts. Let's examine this style more closely:

Piano Clef 1/2+3/4

The piano and organ staves are polyphonous (any staff that divides into two clefs with a plus sign is polyphonous like 'piano 1+2 / 3+4'). Use the above staves, even if for a different instrument, or construct a polyphonous staff. To do this, take a non-polyphonous staff and add channel assignments in Score Styles as you see in polyphonous staves. Set the beams of the note accordingly up or down to separate the parts, all soprano up, all alto down etc. so you can see which part it belongs to. Use the separation tool ![] to place notes in their respective parts if they are misplaced. You can draw a line around a note(s) to place it in a lower or higher part or you can use it 'as is'.

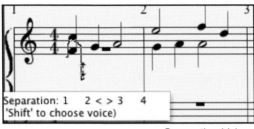

Separating Voices

Decide which parts will show rests for clarity (there are no rests in the example). Select whether you want rests showing for every part. You may insert rests from the part box (the way you choose note values). You may want to insert an eighth rest to establish the value of a dotted quarter note (if not followed by an eighth note it appears as a half note). Your printing can only improve with practice. You must get the experience you need by printing five or six songs. By experimenting with these all of these variables you will soon make your score and parts fit the page and be pleasant to read. It does not take long to learn to print clear scores and parts.

Chapter VIII:
Recording - Basic

Basic Recording to 1 Stereo Channel

Now it is the time to make an actual recording. Your next recording will be better, for you will learn how to enrich the sounds of your instruments and add expression to them in this chapter. You will learn to adjust the tone, tempo and expression in your sequences and various ways of inputting sounds. Some of these enrichments were added to 'Hotcha!'. You can hear the finished recording of 'Hotcha!' on the CD that accompanies this book and see the song in the Appendix II.

Most recordings are made to audio tracks and then put on a CD, or are first recorded to hard disk, bounced to a stereo pair and then burned to a CD. Computer CD recorders are inexpensive and the actual disks themselves are cheap and readily available. A lot is to be learned by recording to a stereo channel first. The idea in basic recording is to record all the tracks (MIDI instruments) at once. In an advanced recording we would record each MIDI instrument or each group of like instruments to separate audio channels, adding the Logic effects in different degrees, and then make a final recording.

Record all of the channels at once to make one stereo file. In both cases we end up with one stereo audio file (interleaved), or a split stereo which consists of two soundwaves, left audio and right audio. We are then able to burn it to a CD, mp3 or record it to a tape.

In both basic and advanced recording, the MIDI instrument sounds are produced by the sound module or sampler or keyboard. We shall simply say sound 'source'. In basic recording, effects are also produced by the sound source. Pan and volume can be controlled from there or by Logic.

The effects can be applied to each instrument within the sound source. What is recorded is a direct mixture of all the modified voices at once.

The advanced method is better, but slower, than the basic method of recording because the audio recording uses Logic's resources, (its native effects like reverb, for example, its pan and volume controls). It allows a greater degree of control because it deals with individual waves, one at a time. In basic recording, the results are as good as your sound source. In advanced recording the audio stream is acted on by the computer itself (Logic) and uses the effects from within Logic.

It is important that you keep this distinction in mind. You may find that basic recording is sufficient for your purposes and you will never have to enter the complex world of audio recording.

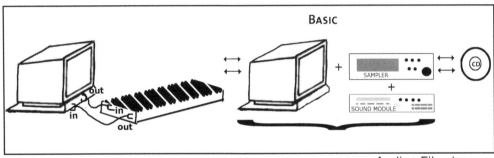

BASIC

| Song is input into Logic tracks with MIDI. | The effects from your sound sources are added here.All tracks are recorded at once to an audio file. | Audio File is burned to CD |

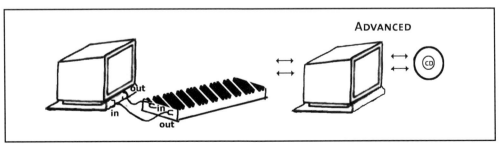

ADVANCED

| Song is input into Logic tracks with MIDI. | Audio tracks are created.Logic effects are added,groups made, busses set to share effects. Audio files with effects are bounced to stereo tracks. | Audio File is burned to CD |

Your First Recording

Look at 'Hotcha!' in Appendix II and listen to it on the CD. This is the Logic song form with all settings just before recording with all empty measures erased, ready to record.

In this chapter you will learn to make a CD and learn how to fatten and differentiate sounds, set up groups, etc; in short, the techniques used in making the CD.

Equipment Connections

Here is the place to talk about how all your equipment should be connected. It might be consulted at the very beginning of the book. Look at the following diagram: you have three types of connections, USB, audio and MIDI. There is a logic (no pun intended) to the connections. If you take a minute to analyse the diagram you should understand it.

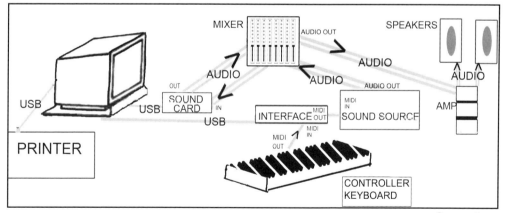

Connections

Outputs

Make sure that your selected (Logic) outputs are connected correctly to your equipment. If they are not you will be recording in vain. I chose outputs 1 and 2 for my recording.

Choose the Track Mixer with [⌘+@/2] and look at the audio 1 channel strip. You will be recording to an audio track, presumably audio track 1, so select your inputs and outputs here.

Choosing Outputs

Audio Path

Press the pre-designated key [A] for audio path. A box appears asking you where on your hard disk(s) you want to keep your recording. Set your audio path accordingly. Many experienced sound people keep their audio recordings and audio programs on separate hard drives, so if you have more than one drive do that as well.

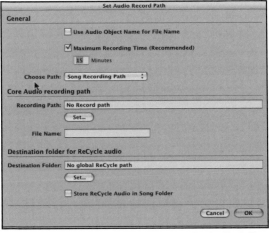

Audio Path Box

Effects and MIDI controllers

On the MIDI track, click on a word at the top of the track, just above the pot. Check it on the image and in real life. Then select the controller number you want to trigger in your sound module and use the pot to set the strength of the effect. Do the same for the other effects and for pan. Replay your song to test the effects. Reverb is controller number 91; pan is set by the lowest round fader on the channel strip. If your module does not contain the effect, reverb, for example, setting 'reverb' in the program will be useless.

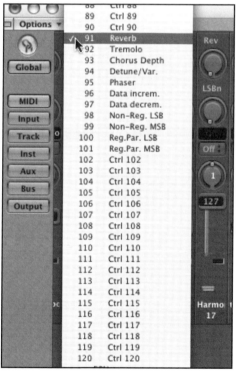

Choosing MIDI Effects

Setting Pan, Reverb and Volume

Set pan and reverb for each instrument separately. Put more reverb, up to 25% on the higher, lead instruments, less on the other instruments, little (5%) on percussion. Set the pan on each instrument about 10 numbers apart, where the instrument would be located in the band in real space, that is on a stage or in a hall, for example. Try to keep lead instruments somewhere in the middle. Play with it until it sounds good to you. We will discuss reverb more thoroughly later, but for now let us just say that you add more reverb the higher the frequency range of the instrument. Bass and drums would then have just a little. Our pan pot sets a zero point and goes to the right and left of zero; some pan pots are strictly numeric starting from number 1.

Next you set volumes. If you set the song to cycle mode and play, there is always something playing while you are testing and that makes the process of testing easier. On the MIDI channels of your track mixer (   ), set pan and reverb or set them up on the channels of your sound modules and synthesizers. Make sure 'global' is switched off and MIDI is switched 'on'. You will see your existing tracks – all of them – so it is good practice to erase the tracks on the Arrange Screen that you are not using (Menu >Track >Delete unused). You can create new tracks when you need them (Menu >Track >Create).

Clicking on the name of the effect on the fader allows you to change it. The knob fader is called in technical lingo a 'pot'. A pot is merely a circular fader (potentiometer), like the volume of a more traditional radio. It governs the strength of each effect. As mentioned, your sound source may not have some of the effects you want. It all depends upon your sound source. If you do not get the desired effects on yours, beg or borrow one for the purposes of making the recording. Be aware that any sound source may contain sounds which may not mix well together.

Arming the track

Before testing you must 'arm' the audio track for recording by selecting the 'R' on the track and make sure that the inputs selected within the track correspond to your physical connections. Press play and keep the volume reasonably low, where it sounds good, so you do not produce distortions in sound. You may make lots of fader volume changes while your song is playing. A method for reducing this work by grouping the faders will be shown next chapter. Later you can use a compressor in order to control volumes and avoid distortions.

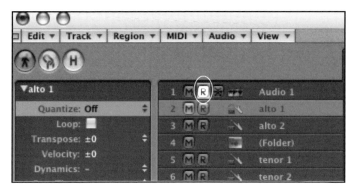

Arming the track

Record

Once the effects and volumes have been established, as mentioned in the previous section, stop playback and return to bar 1 by pressing stop again. Press ✳ or the record button on the Transport Bar to engage record. You will be recording in stereo. The stereo button is to the left of the recording button. Set the volume on the audio fader of the track you are recording to. Each audio track has an up and down audio fader; track 1, called 'audio 1', is activated by audio fader 1, track 2, called 'audio 2', by audio fader 2, and so on. The song will play in real time and you will record it to the audio track. If you have set the volume to sound good, it should not take many attempts to set a level that you are satisfied with. If you see red in your fader, it means that the volume is set too high and has caused distortion, called 'clipping'. Erase the recording and turn the volume down a bit. Do it again. Adjust the volume until the red disappears.

Distortion

You do not want the soundwave to exceed the sides of the track. This indicates that you are recording at too high a volume. You receive a message that clipping (distortion) has occurred. If red appears on the channel strip, distortion has occurred. In that case, you would delete the wave by selecting and backspacing (or under 'edit' menu select 'undo recording'), and record again. You avoid clipping by lowering the volume on your sound module or sampler while recording.

If you find clipping (and the program will tell you so), reduce the volume by a little more than the amount you have distorted. The channel strip will show by how much your sounds have exceeded 0dB, which should be your maximum. Correct (reduce) the volume by a little more than that amount. If distortion reads -6.5 then make the distance between good recording and distortion at least -6.8 dB or -6.9 dB. Headroom, the margin between nominal operating levels and distortion levels, is usually set to about 0.3 dB below the the point where distortion occurs. Your recording level on the fader should show only yellow. If red shows and a number appears on the fader, you have created a distortion. The number shows by how many dB you have distorted up to 6.0 dB.

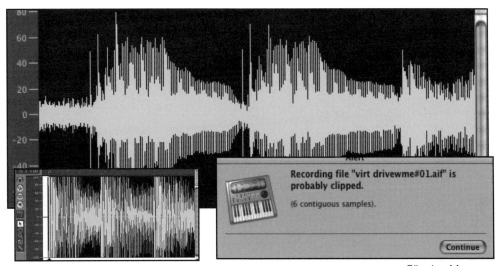

Clipping Message

Amount of Distortion

You can hear each of the instruments in the recording by first muting all the MIDI tracks by a Command click on any 'M' for mute and then unmuting by clicking the 'M' of the audio track you want to hear. Press one of the commands for 'play' (the space bar, 'play' on the transport bar) to play the audio track.

When you are satisfied that there is no distortion, you erase your trials and set the SPL at the beginning of your song. Make sure the audio track you want to use for recording is selected. Press 'record' and make your final recording.

If you are going to make a CD of your recording you should make sure that you select 16 bits and 44.100 kHz stereo. Set these by selecting 'bounce' on the mastertracks at the far right end of the track mixer or by File >Bounce. Under Audio >Sample Rate choose 44100 and then > check '24 bit recording' in Audio >Audio Hardware & Drivers.

On the audio track of your Arrange Screen that you have chosen to record to, as you record you see a soundwave emerging. This is the (audio) recording of your instrument. As the recording progresses you will see a representation of the actual soundwave unfold on your screen and when it is finished recording you will have a soundwave saved to Logic.

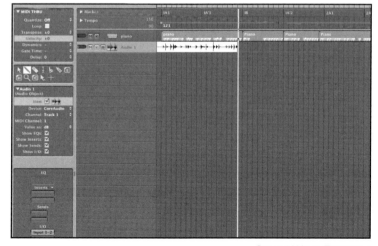

Sound Wave Emerging

For a better look at the wave in detail, open the >Sample Window in the menu choice Audio. You see the soundwave in two forms: in large in the middle of the editor and in small the same soundwave at the top. You can enlarge the wave by enlarging the track. You can play the wave by clicking on the speaker cone icon.

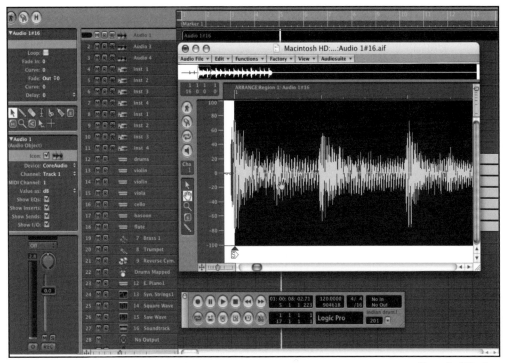

Sample Window

Further recording to CD

You have just made an audio recording of your song. It can be saved as: a '.wav', '.aiff' or '.SDII' file, called something like audio 1,10. It is what can be seen in the Sample Window. For disc burning these filetypes are interchangeable. Put a disc in your CD burner and then follow your CD burner's software instructions on making a CD. Every CD recorder is different, but all of them ask you to drag the file to the recording area of the program. Do that and soon the CD is merrily being recorded.

All your basic recording discs are made like that, in addition to some techniques discussed in this chapter. This may be enough for your purposes and you may never make a more complicated recording. But you know that there is more in reserve if you ever have to arrange a commercial, show or movie.

Improvements

Most people make their final recording on CD via an audio track so that it can be distributed to artists, film people or agents, or perhaps be uploaded to a website. Before we record, however, we want to make our music sound as good as possible. You can use basic or advanced techniques to record to audio and then burn to a CD or MP3. That is, you can record all your MIDI instruments at once using the effects of your sound source and then make your CD (basic recording), or you can record each instrument and mix more carefully using Logic's effects (advanced recording). Remember, that in either case you are making actual soundwaves on your audio tracks in the same way you are making soundwaves when you are re-recording to other media.

The most obvious first step to any recording is to make a working copy of your basic arrangement and label it Mysongsound.lso. If you make changes that you ultimately do not like, you can start over. It is a good idea to save different versions many times along the way as backup copies. Alternatively you can use the 'Revert to Saved' feature, delete the present song and call up the most recently saved version. I like to have many copies, saved at different times, to rely on.

We are going to look at some basic techniques in sound enrichment. Good work means good editing. One is reminded of the old motto that this work is 'ten percent inspiration and ninety percent perspiration'. Take heed!

Multiple Layering of Instruments

To maximize the quality of sound that can be achieved, we have to make the best use of the instruments we have. How do we achieve this? One way is to enrich or fatten sounds of the instruments by playing different versions (sounds or samples) of the instrument simultaneously. You can use several different mediocre sounding trumpets to make one really rich sounding trumpet; allocate them to different instrument tracks, one to a track. Assign the same score part to different channels so that they play 'all at once'. The idea is to mingle their sounds so that you hear only one instrument.

We will make an example of the trumpets, but it can apply equally to trombones, tubas, saxes or violins. So when you read 'trumpet' what is really meant is 'any instrument'.

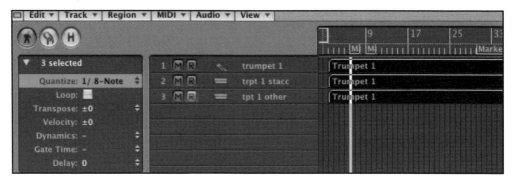

Layering Trumpets

Multiple Layering to strengthen attack

The part of the sound that enables us most to tell one instrument from another is the attack. You can create a stronger attack by mingling a staccato trumpet with your 'regular' trumpets. Load a new song. Input some quarter notes in treble clef leaving a quarter rest between each note so that the attacks can be clearly heard. Have this played by one of your trumpets. Drag-copy the same trumpet part to another track by pressing 'Alt' when dragging, creating two identical parts. Assign the staccato trumpet to a different channel and play the two at once. The first part of the attack of the staccato trumpet particularly emphasizes the attack.

Play the normal trumpet with the staccato trumpet, then without it. Vary the volumes and velocities of each of the trumpets, playing them together, at first making the staccato equal to the other trumpet sound, than gradually soften the staccato. You will reach a point at which the attack does not seem exaggerated and the sound seems satisfying. This is a good way of enriching your trumpet sound. Be sure to include a staccato sample along with a normal sample for all the brass instruments.

If you do not have a staccato trumpet you can make one by modifying the staccato trumpet part: select the part, then select the Matrix Screen in >Windows >Matrix Edit or ⌘+⁶ . Select all (Edit), then shorten a note by pushing on its end until it is about 1/32 of an inch long. It will sound very staccato. You can alter the notes' velocities numerically in the parameter box in Arrange or Score while you are playing the track. You can also create a staccato effect in an instrument using the Event Editor. You could also alter the numbers on the Transform Screen, setting the value to a short note, say a 1/16th note, and fixing the note value.

Add a few more trumpet samples to enrich the sound of the single instrument. Many samples create a single instrument sound. Layering sound upon sound is not my invention; it has been used since the beginning of sampling.

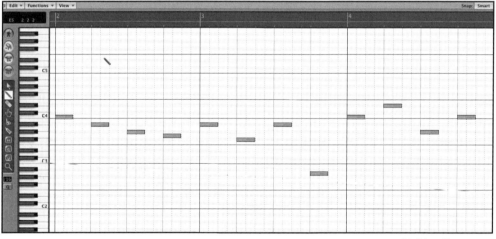

Making Staccatos

Making Tracks

Open the Arrange Screen. Mute all the instruments, audio-instruments and audio objects by command clicking on the 'M' next to any instrument. Then unmute two instrument channels by selecting the 'M' on the instrument track

Make two identical instruments in the Environment (under 'new' menu select 'instrument') and assign the same sound sample to each. Make staves on neighboring channels and tracks of about 10 measures, and create a simple melody of a few measures of quarter and half notes. You have already assigned that channel to using trumpet voice. You now have two identical melodies played by two different trumpets on two different tracks. Save this set up for the next examples but do not save further work so that your Arrange window looks like the illustration.

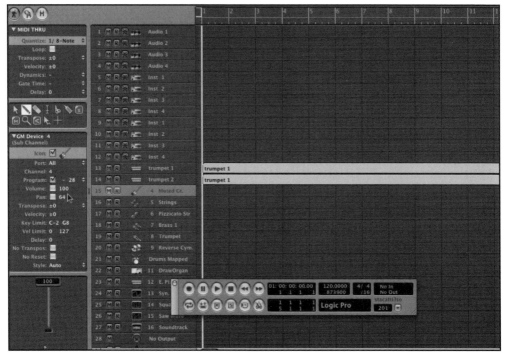

Experimental Set Up

Detuning

Detuning and delaying broadens the sound and makes it sound thicker and hence 'richer' to the listener. You detune by making one channel slightly higher or lower in pitch than the other ('out of tune' with the other). A control on one channel of the MIDI sound module makes it higher or lower than the other channel. This control will have something to do with 'pitch'; some modules allow you to change both fine pitch and coarse pitch.

Detuning is done in the same way on different modules, you just have to find the detuning control of the module. Find it and change the pitch on one channel until you hear the instruments as 'out of tune', then back down so that you are producing one rich instrument, not two instruments 'out of tune'.

On my Roland JV-1080, I move the cents slider for one instrument to a reading of about twenty cents. You will hear a difference. Play the two together and apart, with greater and smaller differences between them. You will find that this procedure broadens the sound a bit and enriches it. If you hear two instruments you have detuned too much. If you had not detuned one of them you would have heard them as one. If you had used a different trumpet voice for each instrument, there would be no point in detuning. In summary, you should experiment with how much to detune to create a rich effect. Too much detuning is unpleasant.

Delay

You have not saved since you were beginning to 'fatten' the sound, that is, you had two identical tracks. Boot up the same song again (which was saved at this point). Another way of 'fattening' identical sounds is by delaying one sound slightly.

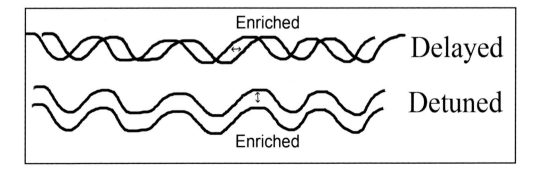

On the Arrange Screen top left, you can introduce delay in ticks. There are 3840 ticks per measure, so if you want to delay one sound 20 ticks, it is the equivalent of 1/192 of a beat. Look at this parameter. Delay one of the sounds and listen to know how much you have to delay a sound in order to thicken ('fatten') it. If you delay too much your song will sound like 'Frere Jacqués', simply not 'in time'.

If you want two trumpets, it is better to use two different sounds than to create one trumpet from another by using effects. You will obtain a more natural sound. Here is that portion of the arrange screen. Experiment with different amounts of delay.

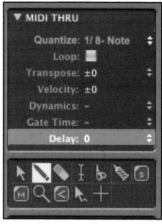

In both cases you are broadening the sound by playing two identical waves but in both cases you keep them slightly apart, in one case by detuning one wave and in the other by delaying one.

Delay on Arrange Screen

Humanize

If you have input a sequence with the mouse it will be perfectly regular, that is the notes will fall exactly on the beat and each note will be held exactly a quarter note in length. One uses the humanize function to de-quantize the sequence so that the sequence is not so regular, so that it sounds like a human played it and not a machine.

If you want to differentiate instruments, humanize them. You use the Transform Screen to do this. If two human musicians played the same melody simultaneously their matrix screens would show that the parts differ slightly. The starting points of some of the notes would be a few milliseconds apart, the volumes and velocities of many notes would be slightly stronger or weaker (different), the phrasing would be slightly different. That is what the humanize function does. It takes a part and causes these differences (transforms it) to be created, even exaggerated, so that the part will sound as though different instruments were playing. Each part is slightly different from the other. The Transform Screen individualizes instruments. This produces a good 'section sound' of many like instruments. If you have six identical trumpets and transform each one, you will produce six trumpets.

If, for example, you have a duet between a clarinet and an oboe, you should humanize both of them to emphasize the sense of having different players. The timing is very different and the separateness of the players is emphasized.

Return to your Arrange Screen. Let us create distinct instruments from one sound sample. Reboot the song, or if you have not saved 'Revert to Saved'' so you have two identical trumpet parts. Create two more trumpet parts using different trumpet voices. Copy the melody to them. You now have four identical melodies (lines). Select a track. Open the Transform Screen by choosing >Window >Open Transform. Click hold the top left drop menu within the window and choose 'humanize'.

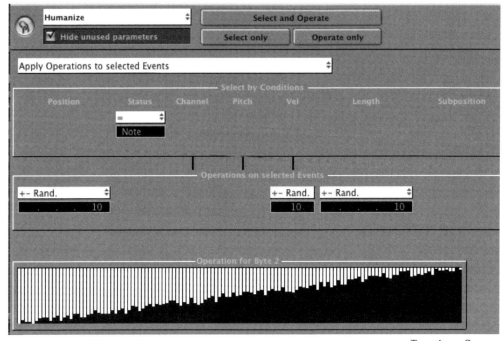

Transform Screen

Humanize each of the tracks except the first one (at the default setting of 10) by pressing 'select and operate'. Then play them together. Do they not sound distinct, like four separate trumpets? While you are playing them together, look at the flashing yellow bars on the tracks. They flash at different times, showing that they are distinct. If you have not played the melody in but input the melody with your mouse, the first track will sound non-human and quantized (more on this below).

Make sure that you add a staccato trumpet to the unchanged trumpet for the sense of attack. Adjust the volume so that the staccato blends into the sound of that trumpet. You want the staccato trumpet to be exactly the same as the unchanged trumpet in timing so the attacks will blend. Therefore you do not humanize them, or, if you do, humanize both tracks together, so that they sound as one.

You can change the degree of difference of each variable on the transform screen but a setting of 10 should be sufficient for randomizing velocities. Use a higher setting of, say, 70 for randomizing the variables of pitch and length. If you want to make the parts more distinct from each other, increase the numbers even more, but listen after each transform so you do not exaggerate too greatly.

In addition to giving a sense of more instruments, humanize is also used for creating a 'section sound' of many instruments when they are playing in unison or soli so that you actually feel that many instruments are playing.

So far we have used detune and delay and multiple layering to produce one instrument sound. If you wish to de-quantize your one instrument, transform all the sounds of your instrument at the same time. If you want to create separate instruments, humanize them separately. This is a new tool in your arsenal, when you get to big band arrangements which call for sections (especially if you have limited sounds).

You decide if you want to 'fatten up' your single instruments or increase the section size. If you have 'played-in' your sequence, you do not have to humanize it. The variations of pitch and length will already be there and you will not have to worry about de-quantizing. If you are using multiple layering to create one 'fat' instrument, Alt drag to make identical copies of your sequence and blend.

Special Effects

This is a digression from basic recording and enriching instruments, but you have come so far that you will need this technique to help impart realness to your scores. You can use multiple layering for every instrument; strings, other brass, and woodwinds. You will also need to create separate instruments for the other special effects, flutter-tongue in trumpets, for example, or plunger wah-wah.

Choosing Effects,Muting Unwanted Lines

Creating Special Effects

This is especially important where you want to add life to a horn line with swells and falls. You set up similar tracks with swelling horns (be they trumpets or trombones or saxes) and separate tracks with the horns falling and rising and then use them when the music requires it.

You can see that an arrangement for a small five-piece combo can have thirty or forty tracks, several for each of the samples that comprise each instrument, especially the lead instruments, playing together, and several for individual effects.

You play all the trumpet tracks but print only one of these tracks. That is why you create separate songs for printing and recording. Or you use Logic's hide button on each track (recent versions of Logic).

Hide Buttons

To turn on this feature you click on the H next to the link button. The button will turn blue. This enables you to see the Hs on all tracks. You can hide a track with H by pressing the button within the track and then press on the big H button AGAIN, to activate hiding (the button will turn to orange), but it still plays. To make the track invisible to playing and viewing, you use the 'M' button.

Use Instrument Sets to separate groups of instruments from all of the instruments for ease in working and printing. You have already assigned ⌘+ctrl+I   to Instrument Sets.

You can configure Logic to open the score by default when double-clicking on a sequence. You do this by Logic Pro >Preferences >Global >Editing.

It helps to make a visual representation track for printing, not playing, which combines the various trumpets into one part with text annotations of *espressivo, tremulo* or the like or use annotated markers. With MIDI you have to create separate instruments for the sounds you want.

Program Changes I - Recording

For every effect you have created a track. Although there may be only three measures of flutter tongue, you have created a track and assigned a flutter tongue sample to it. You will find that you have a lot of non-printing tracks. This can be avoided if you use the technique of program changes.

Pause Record

Program Box

Program changes are used when you only have a few bars of an effect, say *tremelo* violin, in your entire string quartet. In this case you would not want to devote a whole track to *tremelo* violin. You can insert a program change to the *tremelo* violin for a few bars and then change back to another instrument (usually another violin voice).

You can insert a program change in several ways. First, get in record-pause mode by first selecting the Pause button on the Transport Bar and then the record button. Find the location of the bar where you want the change to take place. In the instrument parameter box you wish to change remove the x or check from the Program box if one is present. Move the SPL to where you want the program change to occur. Enter the program number of the sound you want to change to and the location of its port on the MIDI interface (Unitor 3 or Midiman 2 for example) in the parameter box. Check the program box. The program change will be registered and will be duly noted in playback. Then remember to turn off record by pressing the stop button on the transport or the keyboard.

Program Changes II – The Event List

You can also insert program changes using the event list. Move the SPL to where you want the program change to take place. Open the Event List with Windows >Event List. Make sure the show program changes button [88] is illuminated as below. Command click on the program change button. This creates a program change at the position of the SPL. The measure box is automatically opened and you can change the measure of the program change here. Select the number under 'VAL' to change to the voice (program) you want. If there is an existing program change, just command click on either the word 'program' in the event editor or on the program change button. The measure and program change is duplicated. Just change the measure number to where you want the program change to take place and 'VAL' number for the voice you wish to change to. The event will move to the location of the new bar number.

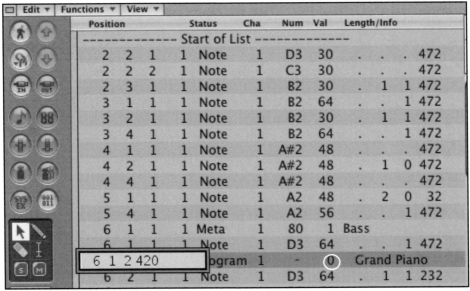

Position				Status	Cha	Num	Val	Length/Info			
------------- Start of List -------------											
2	2	1	1	Note	1	D3	30	.	.	.	472
2	2	2	1	Note	1	C3	30	.	.	.	472
2	3	1	1	Note	1	B2	30	.	1	1	472
3	1	1	1	Note	1	B2	64	.	.	1	472
3	2	1	1	Note	1	B2	30	.	1	1	472
3	4	1	1	Note	1	B2	64	.	.	1	472
4	1	1	1	Note	1	A#2	48	.	.	.	472
4	2	1	1	Note	1	A#2	48	.	1	0	472
4	4	1	1	Note	1	A#2	48	.	.	.	472
5	1	1	1	Note	1	A2	48	.	2	0	32
5	4	1	1	Note	1	A2	56	.	.	1	472
6	1	1	1	Meta	1	80	1	Bass			
6	1	1	1	Note	1	D3	64	.	.	1	472
6 1 2 420				bgram	1	-	0	Grand Piano			
6	2	1	1	Note	1	D3	64	.	1	1	232

Changing Programs with Event List

The other events that can be changed are all easily viewed. There is an array of buttons where each button shows a particular kind of event. I use mostly the note and progam change display buttons. Mastering their use is not difficult.

'Playing-in' Notes

There are real benefits to playing-in the parts on scores that you create as opposed to inputting with the mouse. With playing, you add a human element, a 'liveness' over and above that given by the techniques mentioned above. As mentioned, you will not have to humanize your sounds if you play each instrument individually. If you use your mouse alone to place music for sound reproduction you will have to humanize to get rid of the 'mechanical' sound. Of course if you are interested only in printing you can use any method for note entering.

You can also use the cycle recording technique to 'play-in' notes while recording the tracks in your song. Make sure the instruments are installed correctly on both the Environment MIDI Instruments and Arrange screens. Cycle the measures of the sequence you are going to record. Turn on record.   Then make recording passes with each instrument until the recording is completed. You are not only controlling the accuracy of the notes but also, by playing loudly or softly, the volume of each note. This will save you time later on when you get to mixing and adjusting volumes.

If you miss something in your recording, you can record and add bit by bit to the recorded track.   Be sure to check under File >Song Settings >Recording that 'Merge new recording with selected region' is checked 'on'. 'Click while recording' can be either 'on' or 'off'. You can also reach this screen by click holding the metronome button on the transport bar and select 'Recording'.

Drag-copying

The multiple parts do not need to be recorded separately. They can be copied in Arrange by using select and Alt-drag. The notes can then be edited in the Score Screen with Command Keys. The notes of the doubled parts can also be copied using the same technique. 'Doubling' in this case refers to having two or more instruments playing the same part (e.g. cello and bassoon or at the octave clarinet and bassoon) or multiple layering of two versions of the same instrument (e.g. staccato trumpet and straight trumpet), as well as to the baritone sax playing the same melody as the alto sax. Make sure you adjust the clefs for transposing instruments.

Note Correction

Interpretation

Nobody plays perfectly. What you think may be a cleanly played sequence actually has notes held down with previous and following notes, so-called overlaps or notes that are just a little bit too long or a little bit too short. Turning interpretation 'on' in the score can avoid an overly precise notation of every rest, but even that is not sufficient.

Interpretation Off

Interpretation On

Quantization

Another defect is that sometimes some of the notes may sound as if they are not held long enough, or that all of the instruments do not stop and start at the same time. Sometimes the notes have to be brought in line so that they start and stop at the same time in the Matrix.

These problems can be resolved by quantizing in the Matrix Screen. If very few notes need to be corrected you can change the note lengths manually. For example, if you want these notes to start on the (quarter note) beat, just select and quantize them to the quarter note beat. The sequence that I played in was not even; most of the notes did not start exactly on the beat. I quantized the notes so that they would start at the quarter note position of every beat in the bar. If several parts are quantized to the same beat it guarantees that the notes will start at the same time. You have to be careful about long quantized passages. They are timed so perfectly that they tend to sound artificial. You can humanize them or make them 'imperfect' by moving the notes of the Matrix Screen.

The grid, or amount of time by which the note bars move, is set on the Matrix Screen. I usually set the grid to maximum (192) and adjust by the senses: ear and eye. Remember that fine adjustments of the note lengths are possible with
[ctrl] ,or if you want to make even finer adjustments hold down [ctrl] + [⇧] as you drag. Remember to put the grid back to 1/16 or 1/8 for shifting time positions with the arrows. Previously I have pointed out the place on the Matrix Screen where you set the grid.

Sometimes when viewing several parts in Matrix, a note from one part covers another note. Point on the covering note and temporarily move it elsewhere, in order to get at the covered note. Viewing a part singly in Matrix, then double-clicking anywhere on the window display to see all of the parts, is a method that helps. You can also click on the square at the window's top left corner to bring up all the parts.

Unquantized

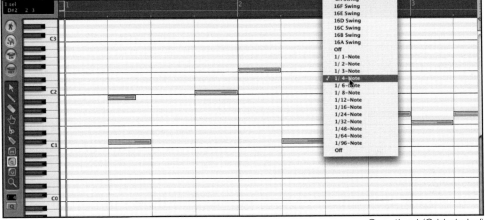

Quantized (Grid circled)

If you have selected a single staff, you get a visual display of that staff in the Matrix Screen. It might be convenient in some cases to set up several matrix single screens side by side. To make multiple screens make sure that you reduce the screens in size so that they do not overlap. If they overlap and you click on one, the screen you clicked on will remain, the other will go behind it or disappear. To be useful, the link icon should be set to off. Using the 'Tiling Screens ' command is a good habit to acquire, or you can open additional matrix windows by holding 'Alt' when selecting matrix edit from the 'Windows' menu. The window will open as a floating window which will NOT disappear when you select another window within the screenset.

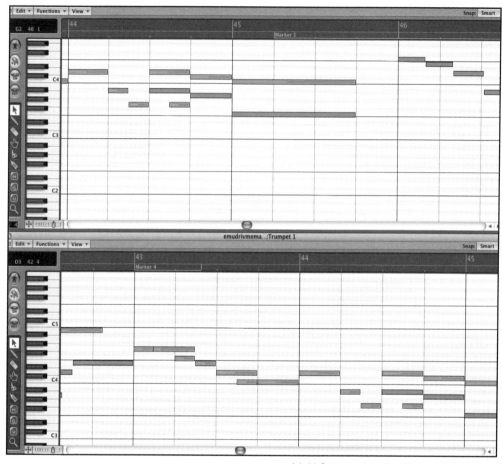

Multi Screen showing Two Matrix Editors

Force Legato

One important way of altering the notes is by making a passage legato. This means that the notes flow into one another, the next note beginning where the previous note ends. This can be done with the menu choice >Functions >Note Events >Note Force Legato or by setting up a key command for force legato. 'Selected/Any' forces legato for all selected notes REGARDLESS of whether the following note is selected or not. 'Selected/Selected' forces legatos for all selected notes but the following note MUST be selected. Experiment with a passage while you are in Matrix so that you can see how this command affects the notes.

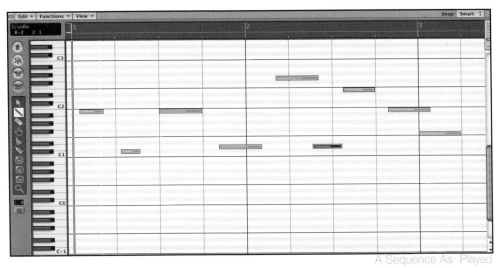

A Sequence As Played

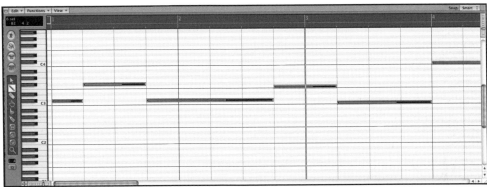

A Sequence With Forced Legato

Correct Overlap

Overlap occurs from 'overholding' one note while playing another. It is a very natural slip of the finger, but hard to correct in playing. It is, perhaps, easier to correct in the program. Often overlapping of notes creates a muddy sound, especially when one chord plays while another chord is already playing.

If a note overlaps with a note of the same pitch, you will hear it as one note. You have a special overlap correction for notes of the same pitch. For the rest you can correct all notes with the menu command Functions >Note Events >Note Overlap Correction.
'Selected/Selected' and 'Selected/Any' work as they did in 'Force Legato'.

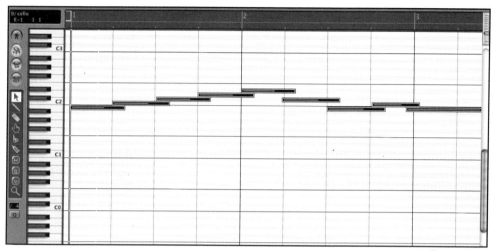

Overlapped

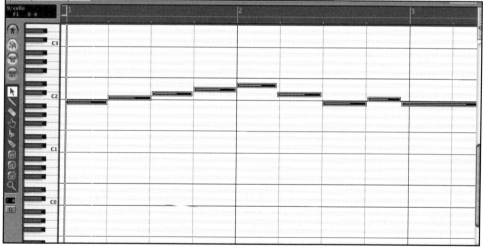

Overlap Corrected

You can see this effect best by inputting a dozen notes, changing to the Matrix Screen and observing the effects of each command. Use the undo feature (Command Z) frequently to check the before and after screens.

Other Matrix Screen Corrections

The Matrix Screen can be used for other purposes. Sometimes you do not want a strictly legato effect. Use legato frequently, but not automatically. It is a question of personal taste.

Sometimes you want a very legato effect. You can make an instrument sound very legato by making the notes overlap slightly. This is especially effective with strings passages or string glissando runs. It is a typical violin sound, used frequently; you will recognize it.

First, make the passage legato with Force Legato. Then in the Matrix Screen manually select all of the notes and drag and push just enough to have one note overlap the other. Or, if you are a good keyboardist, temporarily set the tempo very slow and play in the passage overlapping the notes. (Then reset the tempo to where it was.)

There is much that can be done in the Matrix Screen. You can change velocities by clicking the note with the velocity tool. Drag down for low velocities, drag up for high velocities (notice the note's color change as you drag) . Personally I prefer working with that parameter in numbers in the Score Screen. You can move, add, and delete notes using the Matrix Screen or make those changes in one of the other editing screens. Whether you effect a lot of changes from here or not, it will pay off in easier arranging to becoming fluent in your use of the Matrix Screen.

Expression

In making your music sound good the most important word is expression. This is a broad topic dealing with the interaction of tempo, volume and the entire tone envelope. Although expression deals with the interaction of these variables, we will have to dissect them one at time.

Logic offers you many ways to assign duration and velocity to the diacritics used in expression, where you assign a certain length, say of 15% and a Velocity, say of 20, to >, and lesser length, say 10% and a velocity of, say 10, to <. These are accents and the velocity and length assigned is in addition to those already assigned to the note. MIDI meaning is useful to those who input their notes with a mouse; I prefer to play in my accents.

Number of Layers

The number of layers depends on the quality of the samples. Very often lead instruments use several samples; accompanying instruments do not. If the brass instruments have a strong attack you do not have to create a staccato track. The same is true for delay and detune.

Expression - Adding meaning to accents

This deals with the way in which the voices are used. Here is where considerations of note length and volume enter in as well as voice quality. This combination of qualities is suggested by written accents. Accents are used a lot in jazz arranging, especially for the saxes. In orchestral writing they are everywhere. Each accent refers to a combination of duration of the note and its loudness.

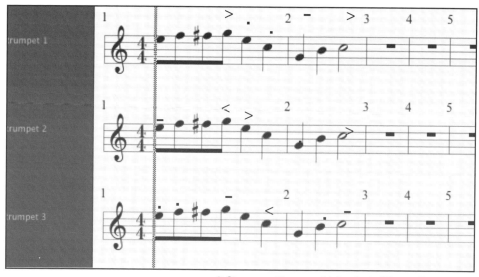

3 Staves with same Notes but different Expression

The same notes in the above phrases are played differently, depending on the length or velocity assigned them. We indicate expression by traditional notation, '>' for a bit longer and loudest note of the group, '<' for accented but softer than '>', and ' - ' for louder (accented), but not as loud as '>'. Finally, the note with the staccato indicates extreme shortness, but no indication of loudness. This is to show you how important it is to indicate the expression you want.

Logic can create music with expression in a number of ways. I prefer to use 'playing-in' to do this. We shall mention other ways for completeness of discussion. The basic idea is that some notes are played shorter and softer and that others are played longer and louder. Keep in mind that the result is the same, just achieved differently. Let's examine the many ways of doing this.

Method 1. – The Accents

You will find these accents, as mentioned above, in all music, especially in big band arrangements. You can assign meaning to these accents and then place the accents on a phrase. In version 7 it is: File > Song Settings >Score >MIDI Meaning. Here you assign loudness and duration for each accented note, the way a musician does when playing.

Method 2. The Matrix Screen

First an unmarked (without accents) phrase is written and then modified by means of the Matrix Screen. Differences in length, velocity and duration are introduced here.

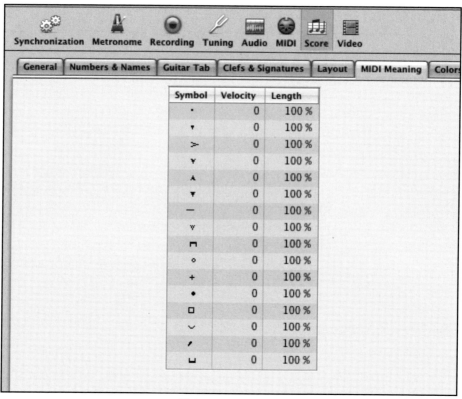

Symbol	Velocity	Length
.	0	100 %
ˇ	0	100 %
˃	0	100 %
˅	0	100 %
˄	0	100 %
▼	0	100 %
—	0	100 %
˅	0	100 %
⊓	0	100 %
◇	0	100 %
+	0	100 %
●	0	100 %
□	0	100 %
⌣	0	100 %
✓	0	100 %
⊔	0	100 %

Giving Meaning to Expression Symbols in the program

Add changes to length and velocity with the matrix editor. Remember to set the grid to fine (192). Shorten and lengthen your notes. Then change their volume with the volume tool. First select the note or notes and the velocity tool. Drag the mouse upward or downward over the note to change the velocity. Check the info line to see the exact velocity. You will find it helpful at this point to use the cycle command to play and listen to each change. If the phrase sounds good but does not stand out (is not loud enough), you can adjust the entire level using a mixing fader and still maintain the relative velocities among the notes.

Using the Matrix Screen

Method 3. Change numerically in Score.

Open the Score and find the phrase to be changed. Select the notes you want to be louder. Assuming that the background instruments will be set to 50, make the selected notes louder than 50. Set the velocity to approximately 75, by dragging on the velocity number. Play with the settings until you are satisfied with the sound. Again, this phrase can be adjusted using the mixer at a later stage.

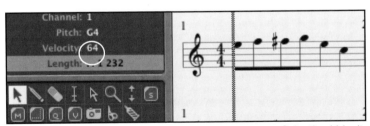

Selecting Velocity

Later, when you go to the mixer, the relative sound level distances between the notes will be maintained, i.e. if you make the volume louder (increase the gain of the whole phrase), you will still hear a difference in relative loudness or softness (velocities) in the notes of the phrase.

You can change the velocities by this method, as you just did and the note length by playing or with another method, such as the matrix. Do not forget that every change made on any screen is reflected in every other screen. I usually set velocities with the Score Screen and durations with the matrix screen. The duration of the note can also be changed numerically in score, although it is easier to change duration in Matrix.

Method 4. The Event Editor

Position				Status	Cha	Num	Val			Length/Info	
----------				Start of List	----------						
1	1	1	1	Note	1	E4	64	.	.	1	232
1	1	3	1	Note	1	F4	64	.	.	1	232
1	2	1	1	Note	1	F#4	64	.	.	1	232
1	2	3	1	Note	1	G4	64	.	.	1	232
1	3	1	1	Note	1	E4	64	.	.	3	197
1	4	1	1	Note	1	C4	75	.	.	1	208
2	1	1	1	Note	1	G3	64	.	.	3	168
2	2	1	1	Note	1	B3	60	.	.	3	208
2	3	1	1	Note	1	C4	64	.	1	3	232
----------				End of List	----------						

Changing Velocity or Duration with the Event Editor

A more cumbersome method of velocity or duration change is with the event editor. I use the Event Editor for changes of contiguous notes, because you can change many notes at one time. Changes are made by click dragging on the appropriate number.

Method 1, assigning value to accents and using them, I find rather cumbersome. Write the diacritics only as symbols. I use Methods 2 and 3 frequently, Method 4 hardly at all. I usually play the accents in with changes in loudness and duration and later write them as text without assigning aural (MIDI) meaning to them.

In the Event Screen you can view the numerical changes made in the score screen and the length changes made in the Matrix screen.

Changes of expression over a larger area

Hyperdraw

We touched on Hyperdraw in an early chapter about Logic's organization. A more detailed discussion is in order here. Hyperdraw is a facility for drawing a change contour under a sequence (on a track). This contour can influence volume, panning, pitch bend, a whole variety of features. This form of expression change can extend over a larger contour than just a few notes.

In Arrange, select a melody track. Make the track about an inch deep (2.5 cm.) with `ctrl` + `↓` . Select View >Hyperdraw >Volume. A blue box appears under the track and as a part of the track. Using the mouse and going from click to click you can visually lay out the volume contour of the melody. You can also draw a contour for other variables, such as velocity, program change and pan, and effect controller changes with breath, if you have a breath controller. The Hyperdraw menu will show the possibilities. The management of controllers is an advanced topic. We will use Hyperdraw mostly for volume and velocity.

Hyperdraw can also be invoked in the Score Screen in the same way, through that screen's View menu. It appears large, at the bottom of the screen.

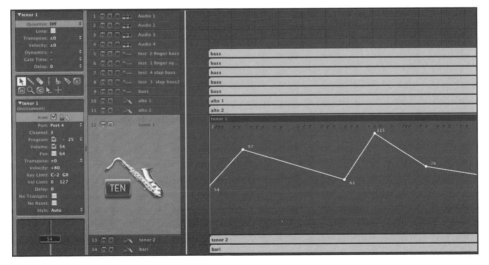

Hyperdraw and Arrange

You can turn off Hyperdraw through that particular screen's View. But whether it is visible or not, Hyperdraw's control continues. If you have Hyperdraw active on both screens and cancel it on one, it will continue to show on the other. So 'off' does not mean 'cancel'; it means only that the contour you have entered cannot be seen. Changes are made to your sequences; you can turn Hyperdraw back on and erase them individually or you can erase all of them at once in HyperEdit. Whether you turn Hyperdraw on or off, the same changes will be visible or invisible but they are always in effect.

The reader should know the difference between velocity and volume. Velocity is the energy with which you play, and we usually hear it as sound level or volume. But if you play drums with energy and then reduce the volume, you still hear how they were played energetically. On the other hand, if you record drums played lackadaisically (without loud energy, i.e. velocity) and then play them back at loud volume, they just sound loud.

Just move your mouse along, clicking on the desired velocity changes. A contour line will unite your choices. If you make a mistake, clicking on the mistaken node will make it go away and you can continue on.

Tempo

Tempo is important to the expressive effect of your arrangement. It adds to the human quality of the music. One thinks of the characteristic lilt of waltz music or the strong off-the-beat feel of Reggae.

There are other natural changes in tempi that we are conditioned to expect. It seems natural that the violins speed up on their runs, and that the ensemble slows slightly upon reaching a conclusion. After the end of the introduction it seems natural to wait for the melody.

In film music the tempi change constantly. You can find four or five tempi in one scene as the emotional content changes. The tempi can be altered by a number of methods. More than one method may be used concurrently, but I find that very complicated and suggest that you stick to one method in any one song.

The basic tempo is shown at the start of the song and at the current moment on the Transport Bar, from the last change to the present. Variations cannot be entered on the Transport Bar. If you change the tempo to 200 at bar twenty, the next time you play it, the whole song will play at 200.

You use one or more of the following methods to introduce your changes:

Method 1. The Tempo List

This is especially easy to use if there is an abrupt change from one tempo to another. In >Options >Tempo >Tempo List Editor you find a screen very much like the event editor. Click on Create and a line representing your original tempo setting on the Transport Bar appears. Change to the desired tempo, then change the first bar number on the far left to the measure where you want the change to begin. The bar orders itself according to this measure number. Change the beat and part of beat numbers to where you want them.

Clicking on the word 'tempo' with the pencil doubles the bar that you click on and takes you directly to the numbers that govern measures and beats. You may prefer to use the pencil. You may make any change you desire, gradual or abrupt.

If you want to get into the new tempo with a little *rallentando,* create a tempo list that looks like this:

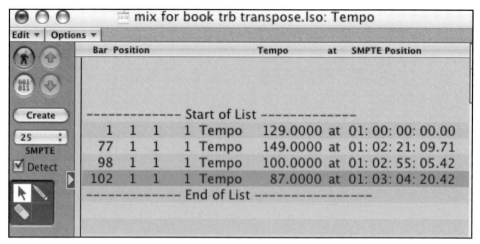

The Tempo List

Method 2.   A Tempo Fader

This is ideal for movie music, where the tempo constantly changes with the mood. Go to the Environment, the 'Clicks and Ports screen'. Choose >New >Fader >Specials >Tempo Control. A small fader appears on the screen. Move it to a clear space and then enlarge and elongate it. You will have to practice how to manuevre the devices. You elongate the fader to make the tempo changes more gradual thus allowing more control over the fader. You will get a message telling you to position the fader between the physical input and the sequencer. You do that cabling the fader as follows:

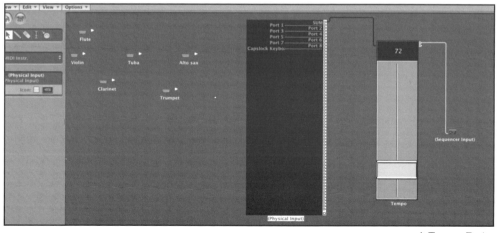

A Tempo Fader

When you record you will want to have your volume faders and your tempo fader. Make a screenset of both of them.

Method 3.   A Tempo Graphic Editor

Those of you with Logic 6 or earlier can use the Tempo Graphic Editor (it is not to be found in Logic 7 and has been replaced by a screen called 'Tempo Operations').   You reach the Tempo Graphic Editor through the menu >Options >Tempo >Tempo Graphic Editor, and then draw with the pencil the levels of your tempi. Lower is slower and higher is faster. The level at which you stop drawing is the tempo that will continue. It is as easy as that. The Tempo Graphic Editor is very much like Hyper Edit applied to tempo. It is a good method for making a gradual transition from one tempo to another as well as making abrupt tempo changes.

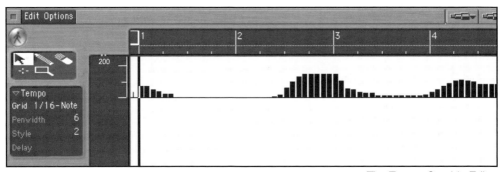

The Tempo Graphic Editor

Method 4. Tempo Operations

This method allows you to make transitions between two tempi; 'where it's changing' and 'what it is changing to'. The screen allows you how to hook these changes up, either through gentle curves or other transitions. It is located in different places in the versions of Logic. In Logic Pro 7 it is located in >Options >Tempo > Tempo Operations.

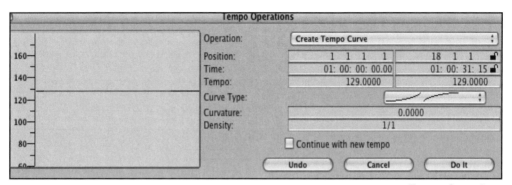

Tempo Operations

Method 5. View Global Tracks

New to Logic 7, this screen gives you two utilities in one. All the tempi of the song are displayed on a track. If you wish to introduce changes, you just pencil-click where and at what speed you want to make the change. The tempo line jumps up (or down) to the change you have introduced. You get to this operation through the Arrange Screen and View >Global Tracks Components >Tempo. You get the same overall view of time signatures, transpositions and markers you have placed.

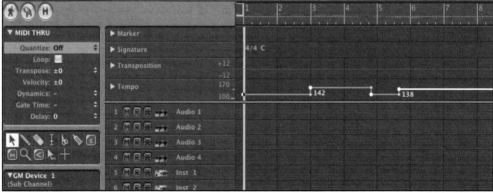

Global Tracks

Making Waves

We have made a CD, where we have bounced all the instruments with their effects directly to a stereo audio track, and then CD. In this chapter we are going to record those instruments to audio, one by one (or in sensible groups of identical instruments), and then mix and record those audio channels, with added effects, to one stereo track, preparatory to making a CD. You will find a few recording tips along the way, like recording in groups, and ways to 'fatten' audio waves, not MIDI instruments as in the previous chapter. You will also learn how busses simplify your work and reduce CPU load.

Finally we will discuss reverb and pan as psychoacoustic cues and where they fit into advanced recording, as well as other Logic native effects.

A Visible Sound Wave

First let us go over what you actually do when you do basic recording in Logic. You record a stereo soundwave to an audio track. First you reduce the number of segments on a track by first gluing them together, then you delete all empty measures. You can reduce tracks further by creating folders within Logic. You choose inputs, and then test your volumes, avoiding distortion.

You are ready to go on to advanced recording. Instead of setting your effects in MIDI, you are going to add Logic's effects to the instrument recordings.

Boot Logic. The Arrange window will open. Mute all the instruments, audio-instruments and audio objects by command clicking on the 'M' next to any instrument or audio object. Create a MIDI instrument and make sure that there is a sound on your sampler or sound module. Unmute a MIDI instrument track and enter the melody of your arrangement (or 'Drive Me Crazy' if you don't have your own). Select and unmute an audio channel. Turn up the volume. [In newer versions of Logic the channel strip of your audio mixer appears at the lower left of your Arrange Screen so you do not have to call up the Track Mixer.] Play your sequence, check your level, then select the [*] button on your keypad or the record button of your Transport Bar to engage record as in Chapter VIII. Record this one track to audio 1

The Advanced Recording Process

The rest of this chapter is divided into initial recording, improvements to the recordings and making a final mixdown. That is the advanced recording process. Interspersed are recording tips and important topics in relation to advanced recording. Please keep this process of advanced recording in mind throughout.

A version of 'Drive Me Crazy' is an advanced recording. Please refer to it on the CD while you are reading this chapter.

Initial Recording

You have made a simple recording to audio 1. The recording is on the track controlled by a channel strip and fader. When you make your advanced recording, you record, one instrument at a time to Audio 1, Audio 2, Audio 3, etc. Now enter the rest of your arrangement (or 'Drive Me Crazy').

Here is how you add effects to the recordings. Use [⌘+2] to call up the track mixer. On the channel strip corresponding to Audio 1 you see a box marked 'insert'.   Experiment with it. If clicked on and held, it gives you numerous effects, both Logic's original effects and core audio effects, developed by the designers of the core audio engine. With select, slide over to stereo effects>Logic>reverb> Averb. Not only is the Averb machine selected, but it is displayed on your screen for you to work with. As you add effects to the channel, the inserts increase to allow you to continue choosing them, up to 15 per channel – fewer in lesser versions.

Choosing An Effect

Pan is selected using the round pan pot. Experiment with your recording, adding different degrees of pan, then different degrees of reverb. We will discuss them shortly, but for now you can think of pan and reverb as placement in space. You may want to acquaint yourself here with the many effects available through Logic.

Clean up of the Arrangement

Before recording the rest of our arrangement, our first task is to check and clean up the MIDI parts we have entered. If you are not interested in differentiating choruses or entries, the segments of each track may be glued together. They can be selected and glued together easily to make one long track by clicking on the instrument track. Make sure you are not in cycle mode. This selects all the segments on that track. Then touch the track (on any segment) with the glue tool.

You have the personal choice of unifying and making whole long tracks, or highlighting the entrances by erasing blank sequences.

Erasing the empty sequences shows all the flourishes, countermelodies, solos and entrances, etc., that you have written into the arrangement, and makes it easier to locate

Pan and Effects

them. You will then find it easier to control the volume and other effects as the arrangement plays. (Reminder: you need to keep the empty segments within the arrangement when you print in order to get a 'professional looking' score for a musician, a score without gaps.)

I use a screenset of the Score and Arrange Screens for this. I find and locate the empty staves in a part. Then I enclose those measures in a locator loop on the Arrange Screen with ⌘+Y and remove them.

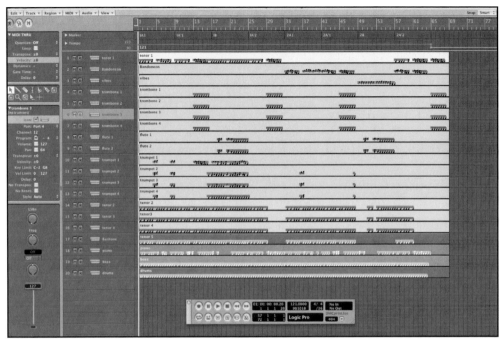

Glued Segments

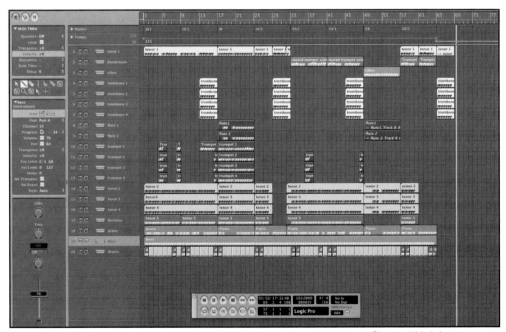

'Cleaned Up' Arrangement

Logic has a neat feature that you can use next to simplify or 'clean up' the arrangement: the folder. Logic groups any tracks you choose into a single track, using the menu Region >Folder >Pack Folder or ⌘+F . The illustration shows the trumpets packed into a folder.

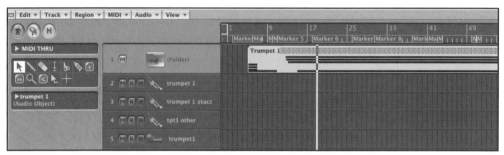

A Folder

This track can be easily expanded into its constituent tracks for editing by clicking twice on the folder. You can return to the Arrange Screen by clicking on the small box at the top left of your screen. You can unpack the folder using Region >Folder >Unpack Folder. You can pack it into the folder and unpack it as many times as you wish.

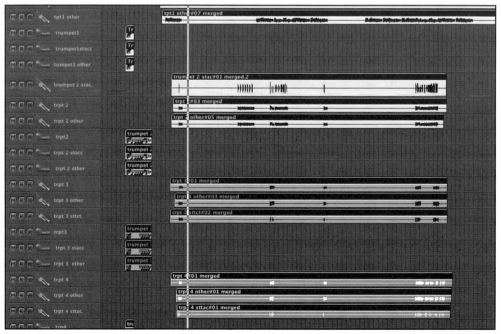

To Be Condensed Into Folders

In a big band arrangement, if you pack all of the trumpets except the lead trumpet carrying the melody, all of the trombones and all of the saxes into single folders you will have a very clean Arrange Screen indeed.

When You Are Recording

Remember, when you record on your own, the goal of advanced recording is to record each instrument or group of instruments, unimproved, to separate audio tracks. After you have set the pan and reverb effects (and any other effects) you record all the tracks again, and mix them together to one stereo track. This will form the basis for your CD or MP3. The final recording is called 'bouncing' to a mastertrack. It can be done in recording mode, and you can change the volumes manually (the 'master volume' fader is also at the far right of your mixer and controls the volumes of all of the channels) or you can make your volumes change automatically and 'bounce' it all at once.

Master Track

You will record each MIDI instrument separately. If you have 25 instruments you should make 25 audio tracks. This is not completely true; piano and drums are recorded in stereo. Some instruments form natural groups. If the trombones play only pads in a fixed chorus you may record them in groups (all trombones, all strings, all woodwinds); one group of like instruments to an audio channel before recording/bouncing all the audio channels to the mastertrack.

Making Tracks

What if you run out of audio objects on the Arrange Screen? In Logic they can always be manufactured. First, you must pre-set the maximum number of tracks available. Select Audio >Audio Hardware and Drivers and set 'Max. Number of Audio Tracks'. I set this number to 24, and add tracks when they are needed.

Here is how you make an audio track: press Windows >Environment and then >New >Audio Object. In the Environment Screen, double-click on the audio object and it will turn into a channel strip. Currently the channel strip is set to 'off'. To change the channel to an audio track, click on the word 'off' in the track parameter box (in the 'channel' row), select 'track' and from the list select a free track number. Use the name tool to change the name of the audio object to 'audio 5' or the next numbered audio object that you need; for example, if you already have audio object 8, rename 'audio object' into 'audio 9'. If you need an audio-instrument, choose 'audio-instrument' from the channel parameter box and when the list appears slide it over to the numbered audio-instrument you want.

If you already have the objects you want in the Environment you can create a new track in the Arrange Screen with [icon] or >Track >Create. Select the kind of track you wish to duplicate. If you have first selected an instrument track, you will create an instrument track with Shift + Return; if you have first selected an audio track you will create an audio track etc. Or if you have any kind of unused track you can convert it to an audio track by selecting and holding on the track name and sliding the cursor over to 'audio track'. It is a good idea to start from a template like combo or big band where you have already put many audio tracks and have chosen your inputs and outputs.

Creating Tracks

You must select on the Arrange Screen the audio track that you wish to record to, otherwise nothing will be recorded; a small but important detail. Remember, you record twice, once from MIDI to audio, then audio with modifications on each channel mixing down to the stereo mastertrack.

Mute all MIDI tracks except the one(s) that you wish to record. If you are going to use multiple layering, either with delay, detuning, or the use of blending several samples, you will want to do so now.

You have already selected your audio path (where you will place your recording) in Chapter VIII. If you haven't, press   now.

Audio Path

Turn on the red record button on the audio track you wish to record. Record one instrument. This is the tricky part, testing the level first, avoiding distortion. Mute the recorded instrument, unmute another instrument and then go through the same procedure. Repeat this procedure until all of the instruments of your arrangement (or 'Drive Me Crazy') are recorded, one to a track, unless, of course, they are stereo. Record all the instruments at a level that sounds natural relative to the other instruments; the leading instruments will be at a higher volume than the accompanying instruments.

As you have seen, the actual audio channel recordings will be complex soundwaves. Sounds in wave-form are easy to enhance and modify. The process of modifying and adding to soundwaves, adjusting the volumes, other characteristics of soundwaves and putting them together is called 'mixing'. When you make your recordings you will be working with many waves at a time, but your ultimate goal is to re-record these audio objects (mix them down) to a stereo pair of soundwaves.

You have recorded all of the instruments, in audio, one at a time. Now we will add some improvements to the individual recordings before mixing. It will improve them considerably.

Improve Each Track

We try to improve each recording (track). You modify each sound by using the effect plug-ins and panorama in the final mixdown, inserting up to fifteen plug-ins on a channel strip in Logic Pro, four in Logic Express.

Next we discuss ways to detune and delay some of the tracks during the mixing stage. Please keep in mind that these are techniques to be employed after the initial recording and before the final mixdown.

Detuning

Duplicate (by drag-copying) a lead instrument's audio track; for example, the trumpet. You now have, on two audio mono tracks, two identical trumpet melodies. To 'fatten' them you are going to make one channel slightly higher in pitch than the other. You do this by putting an effects device on one channel to make it higher or lower than the other.

Press ⌘+2 to get the 'Track Mixer' (with 'global' on) and get into the effect 'Pitch Shifter II' according to the illustrations. Move the cents slider to create a reading of about twenty cents. The whole sequence has been shifted and the effect of the two channels is one 'fattened' trumpet. You can play these two tracks together, one unchanged, one detuned slightly to hear a thicker sound. What makes this 'advanced recording' is that you are using the audio mixer and using a Logic plug-in device to modify the sound.

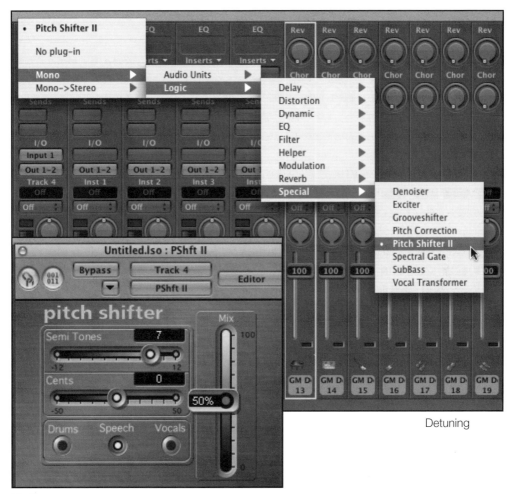

Detuning

Delay

'Bypass' or remove the plug-in to get to where you were before phase shifting, that is, to two identical recordings of the same instrument.

Another way of differentiating identical sounds is by delaying one of them slightly. Use the 'delay' parameter in the Arrange Screen. Play the two and listen to the delay.

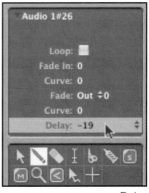

Delay

Special Effects

Reverb and other Effects (FX)

You will describe the placement of the instruments in a two-dimensional space with pan, and describe the placement of the instruments, and the size and composition of the hall, with reverb.

Reverberation or reverb is just one of many effects that can be created by mathematically manipulating the soundwaves. Some effects are: reverb, chorus, equalization and compression. We will talk briefly about reverberation. Mixing and recording are very specialized fields. A lot of technical knowledge, much experience and a pair of great ears are required. We are not going to aspire to those levels. You will add some other effects as you gain confidence and experience. But we will add a little reverb and panorama as essential examples.

Now that you have an existing waveform you can add these effects. They are a part of every arranger's toolkit. We will add just a little reverb to describe the room and panorama to give more life to the location and arrangement of the instruments in the room.

Reverb makes the instruments sound unified and realistic in space by taking the shape, composition and size of the room into account. It also describes the fore-and-aft locations of the instruments in a room. Clearly, a flute played in a huge hall will sound differently than one played in an intimate space. Reverb adds depth, placement in space near or far. How does it happen? By giving us psycho-acoustic cues that signal depth. In sound jargon it pushes back the sound. Imagine being in a big cave. A listener at the mouth of the cave can place your location in it from unconscious cues such as the amount of echo, the size of the cave, the smoothness or absorptiveness of the walls.

The sound depends on reflections of the sound bouncing off the walls and the timing of these reflections. In a large room the time between bounces is longer. Panorama or pan also helps to locate the instruments in terms of left/right placement relative to the other instruments.

Panorama puts your instruments in a line from left to right. If the piano is in the center leave it at zero. The bass is in the crook of the piano to the right? Try setting it at 10 degrees from the piano for separation. Likewise the drums are to the right of the bass by another 10 degrees, so you set it to 20 degrees right. The horns are usually together in three rows to the right of the drums. For clarity, I would place the trumpets and trombones to the right of the drums, separating the first, second, third, and fourth players by 5 degrees. I would put the saxes to the left of the piano, separating the players by 5 degrees each one. Generally it is considered good engineering practice to put low frequencies, particularly regular ones like kick drum or bass guitar, panned center and to adjust the other instruments around them, which we have not done in this small setting.

Let's examine Logic's least complicated reverb: the Averb.

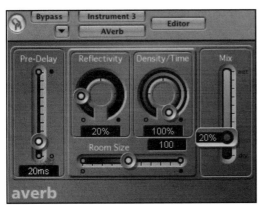 

20% Wet   Wet

'Mix' is how much of the signal will be effected. One speaks of 'wet' versus 'dry' signals. A setting of 100 percent is the wettest. That is full reverb, it will be too much. Dry is a little reverberation. 50 percent is still a lot of reverberation.

'Pre-Delay' is how long, in ms, before the reverb starts. A singer usually requires more pre-delay than an instrument, for example. Pre-delay is also the way in which we adjust how near or far from the listener the sound source is within our virtual space. E.g: pre-delay of 35ms and reverb relativley dry in a medium room gives us a sound that is nearer to us than one rather wetter with a pre-delay of 5ms in the same 'room'.

'Reflectivity' deals with the smoothness and hardness of the walls (and floors and ceilings). You know that your singing sounds different in the bathroom than in the living room. This is partly due to the size but mostly due to the reflectivity of the walls, floors and ceilings.

'Room Size' deals with intimate or public spaces.

'Density' refers to the thickness or washed out quality of the reverb.

You have to play around with these variables singly and together to arrive at your reverb mix. Generally the lower instruments like bass or drums do not need much reverb. Higher instruments like trumpet, altos or clarinets do. If we are adding reverb to the whole ensemble we should add only a small amount. Give each lead instrument its own reverb and to calibrate each reverb to taste. You might have to change pan or volume after adjusting reverb and conversely. If you are dealing with a larger ensemble we will learn to give each instrument its own degree of reverb. We will get to a handy and convenient way of doing this, using the buss, soon.

As you get to know them, you can add other effects like flange or chorus. We have chosen reverb as the most important effect and the one most likely to make your CD sound good. Each effect has its own 'machine', and you will learn what the settings mean.

We try to improve each track in turn. We regulate the volume so as to avoid distortion. We add effects and pan as tastefully as we can. We have restricted our example to reverb, which in my opinion is the most important effect. You will want to add varying degrees of reverb to each instrument.

Freeze Tracks

We have not talked about processor power, but it is a reality of your computer. From version 6 there is a 'freeze tracks' capability to conserve this power. 'Freeze Tracks' creates a temporary recording of your audio track with effects applied. This stops the CPU from having to calculate the mathematical changes each time you play. This keeps the workload down. Even working above the level of this book, with a powerful computer it is

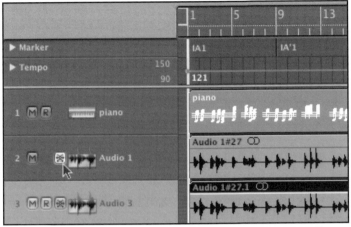

unlikely that you will run out of processing power; but it is reassuring to know that a method for working with more tracks exists when you will need it.

Freeze

The Bus

Busses In Use

It would be more economical in terms of computer resources, and less time consuming, if you used one reverb or other effect unit for several tracks. You do this by using a buss, a device that enables you to control many audio channels at the same time. You select the channels to be effected by sending them to the same bus. Click on the 'insert' slot of one of your bus tracks. Let's put the 'Averb' on 'Bus 1'. Assign each audio track on which you wish to use 'Averb' to 'Bus 1' by clicking and dragging in the 'sends' slot. Little round buttons appear next to the 'sends' on each channel that allow you to set the amount of the signal that each instrument uses.

The bus is used in place of putting the same effect on each track. If you are recording a small group with a small number of tracks, such as a trio or combo, you can place a reverb on each track separately. You can control the amount of reverb to be added on each individual reverb unit. If you are recording many instruments, set the effect(s) up on a buss, and send the amount of the signal to effected from each instrument to that buss.

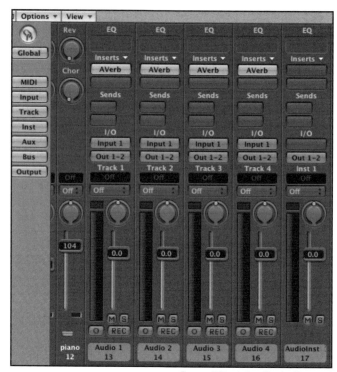

Same Effect On Each Channel

Locate the fader for 'bus 1'. Use the 'Averb' and set the mix up to 100 percent. Since you are regulating the amount of signal you are sending from each instrument with the little round buttons, set the mix to the maximum. If you think that the effect is too strong even when the send buttons are set to a low level, you may lower the 'Mix' level within the effect unit. Leave the other controls where they are. Add a very small amount of reverb to the instruments that you would not ordinarily reverb just to add the flavor of playing in the same hall. You will find that after a bass is given reverb, its volume has to be lowered.

Groups

Now that our entire arrangement has been recorded to audio, and each individual track has been improved, we can start mixing. While mixing you are very busy with the volume faders. For example, you turn the trumpet up for its solo but turn the volume down when it has to blend in with the other trumpets or trombones in the accompaniment. Constantly adjusting a lot of faders is a bother.

Let us cut down on the fader tweaking. We do this in two ways: by grouping the instruments so that one fader works for many; and by recording fader movements. In the first method you only have to adjust one fader and all the faders of that group are 'locked in' and make identical motions. Grouping is a fairly recent feature (since Logic 6), hence it is absent in earlier versions.

First, let us examine this capability in the newer programs. For those of you who can group, it is easy to put the instruments into sections (or other reasonable groups). For example, we put all of the trumpets in one group, all of the saxes together in another group, and all of the trombones in a third group. Instead of juggling twelve or fifteen faders, we only have five or six.

Observe one fader for a trumpet. You will see two boxes just above the volume switch marked 'off'. Click on the upper box. You will be asked which group you want this fader to belong to. Choose a number for the trumpet, say group 1. Go to the fader for the next trumpet. Set that also to group 1. Put all of the trumpets in group 1. Now move one of the faders marked '1'. All the faders in group 1 move together! Put the trombones in group 2. You could put all the brass in one group - at least for a tutti section - or in most arrangements, keep them in several groups. Grouping is very useful in all recording, basic or advanced.

Groups

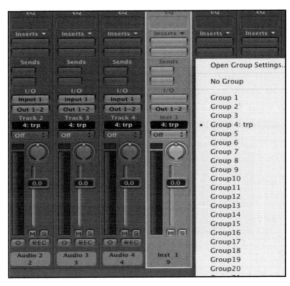

Grouping

MemoMemorizing Fader Movements

This also applies to all recordings and to all versions.

Memorizing Fader Movements

You can mix in real time, where you manipulate the faders as necessary, but it is even easier to mix if you can have the faders memorize their movements before you record. You can memorize the fader movements of one track at a time or of the entire song. I am first going to explain a feature only available in the new versions, then a way to do the same thing in all versions.

On any audio channel strip you see, where indicated, five options, 'Read, Touch, Latch, Write' and 'MIDI'. We will explain them in turn, but first we will actually automate the faders. Select 'Touch' in this box on a fader. Move the SPL to the beginning of the song (0 on the keypad). Play your song. Move the fader up and down during playback. Stop playback and go again to the automation box and select 'Read'. Play the song again while observing the fader. It moves up and down according to the fader movements you have made. You can choose 'touch' for all of your instruments at once if you use the command key.

Here is an explanation of all of the terms in the automation box:

Off: If the automation mode is set to 'off' you will hear the music but without the fader movements you have just recorded.

Read: You set this for Logic to read the fader data you have recorded onto the track. The data is only read; the recording cannot be changed in real time by adjusting the fader.

Touch: This setting automates the track while the fader is being moved. When you stop moving the fader any previous data you have recorded remains. This setting is ideal for your initial movements and later for touching up a track.

Latch: Functions like touch but overwrites everything and when you stop the fader movement you continue to record data wherever the fader happens to be.

Write: Records any data but erases existing data as the SPL passes over it.

MIDI: MIDI cuts off Logic automation instructions and sends MIDI only instructions to the segments. Since we are discussing Logic instructions we will not use MIDI here.

Use ⌘+z to get the song to step backwards to where you were before you entered the volume changes

You can create similar volume changes using Hyperdraw, discussed and illustrated in the previous chapter. We will widen the track for a better view. Select the track line at the lower left of the instrument name. You can widen all of the tracks if you hold the command key down while elongating any one track. When the cursor turns into a pointing finger, click, hold and pull it down. Alternatively, you can widen all of the tracks by using one of the window scale controllers (depending on the version).

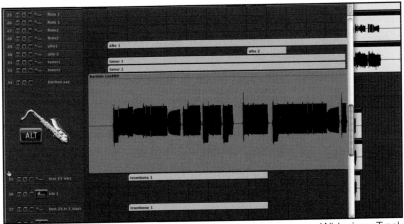

Widening aTrack

From the Arrange local menu, select >View >Hyperdraw >Volume. The selected track will turn blue. You click where you wish to change the volume. The line indicating volume changes as you click. That's all there is to it. Go back to the beginning and play it. The volume changes are all recorded as you indicated.

Final Recording

This is your final mix, your end result. Your final recording is a bounce or a recording of all of the single recordings you have made. 'Bouncing' means recording the many tracks down to one stereo track. You can do this by mathematically and soundlessly creating the soundwave using 'offline' bounce, or you can use record as we have been doing. (You may also select the 'Realtime' option within the bounce window that makes it possible to listen to your mix during the process). Select the 'bounce' button on your stereo output track channel. Both the 'realtime' and 'offline' options take all of the waves, plus all of the enhancements to the waves (the reverbs, the equalization, the panorama), and calculate a wave-form with all of that incorporated in it. A truly wondrous feat!

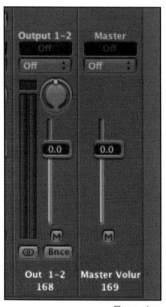

Bouncing

The bounce screen asks you the parameters of your recording, the stop and start positions of the recording, and the add option, (if you want the file in your audio window) what format, and where and under what name you wish to save the file. Just below the 'end' and 'start' position rows you may select the bouncing modes (Realtime or Offline). Bounce. You can select and delete it with your backspace key and try again. You can look at the waveform of your recording in the Audio >Sample Editor window. If your wave looks skimpy it is because of faulty volume settings. You can experiment with degrees of reverb and volume.

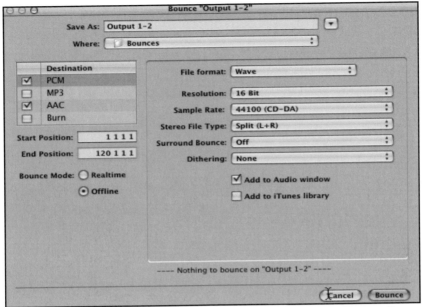

Bounce Screen

Virtual Instruments

In many ways virtual instruments are in between MIDI and audio. Since they are already on a mixer's channel strip, you can use the virtual instruments to first record in your part as you would MIDI, add Logic effects, and then bounce it in the same way you do with an audio track.

The recorded part within the audio-instrument track will look like a MIDI part (which can be treated like a MIDI sequence in terms of notes, events, matrix etc.)

Making a CD

This section is surprisingly short. There are many disk burning programs. Some work only with certain CD drives. At any rate, open your burning program, select your final audio output files in wave form, drag them to the new CD window and record them in .wav format, 16 bit, 44.100 kHz stereo. You can make .mp3 files at varying degrees of sound fidelity, from 320 kbps to 8 kbps. The lower the fidelity the smaller the file. The fidelity you choose depends on the use of the music. You want the highest fidelity possible, except if you have to send mp3 files over the internet. Logic recommends 96 kbps for mono and 160 kbps for stereo.

An ending note

We hope we have introduced you in a painless way to Logic and have taken you through the process of starting from scratch, making an arrangement or a leadsheet of a song, printing it and recording it to a CD. Recording is an art, and making better recordings is a never-ending process. I hope you go as far as you want to with recording. And I wish you many hours composing and arranging with Logic.

Appendix - The CD

Some of the songs in this book are recorded on an accompanying CD. Discussions relating to them and the scores are given here.

A. Again

'Again.lso' is a print of the leadsheet.

B. Hotcha!

This shows what can be done with unison, 3rds and 6ths and how choruses are built, instruments are featured etc. The leadsheet also contains lyrics and chords.

Hotcha! is a simple example of combo arranging with few instruments. I have made the percussion to imitate a washboard with a cymbal attached, hence no drum sounds. I chose a banjo accompaniment for an old time feel. Sometimes the trumpet leads on top, sometimes the clarinet. Notice the variety of simple solos that you can add, especially in the B section. You can make a lot of music with unison or two voices!

Note the copying and repetition of the accompanying instruments. This is a basic recording using more than reverb and pan: chorus is also used.

C. Flying and Feeling So Fine

'Flying and Feeling So Fine' is a basic recording. It was arranged for a small grouping of instruments for a show and really features a sin well as the trumpet. The accompanying instruments were chos smoothness and softness: two tenor saxes and a trombone.

these players a rest and to provide contrast, three clarinets in low register were used; rather extravagant moneywise (and not done in the real world), to get three more players for a small part.

The lyrics are interesting. They are made up entirely of clichés that get more extreme as the song progresses. Remember, the song is intended to be sung. When you hear the bandoneon or see lyrics the singer has entered. Here we have carried the copying and repetition of parts to the extreme. The clarinets play the same spread as the trombones and tenor saxophones.

D. Drive Me Crazy

Many versions of this song are given on the CD.

First, a basic recording of all but the lead instruments is presented to give a picture of the accompaniment. Note that this arrangement was made in the Arrange Screen and the parts for the second chorus and on were copied from the first chorus.

The second version of 'Drive Me Crazy' is also a basic recording. You may contrast this with the third version which is an advanced recording. If the basic recording is 'good enough' for the purpose of your demo, stop here and make basic recordings. Both are made with reverb and pan only and show how far you can go with just the two.

The fourth version is an advanced recording with a full complement of effects: equalization, compression, reverb, pan etc. It is included to encourage you to go further than this book with your recording.
The printed song is also provided here.
I couldn't find a good sample of a baritone sax, so I used a basoon sound instead and it blended well with the tenors and was in the right range. For any given arrangement, experimentation with instruments of similar range and timbre can be used, and I urge you to do so.

I had good samples, so no layering, staccato, detuning or delaying was necessary. The pan places the instruments in their traditional locations (by seating). Reverb was added to give the impression of the depth of placement of the rows, each deeper than the other.

Chorus two shows an example of countermelody – a new, completely different melody is played to the same chords as the first melody, very often done in jazz. This is followed by playing the two melodies against each other, an old arranger's trick.

The second A' was played alone without the usual trombone support. This provided a 'climb down', a restful place before the slower and somewhat elegaic repeat at the end of the song.

Again

81
Clar
tmpt
trb
banjo
85
Clar
tmpt
trb
banjo
89
Clar
tmpt
trb
banjo
93
Clar
tmpt
trb
banjo

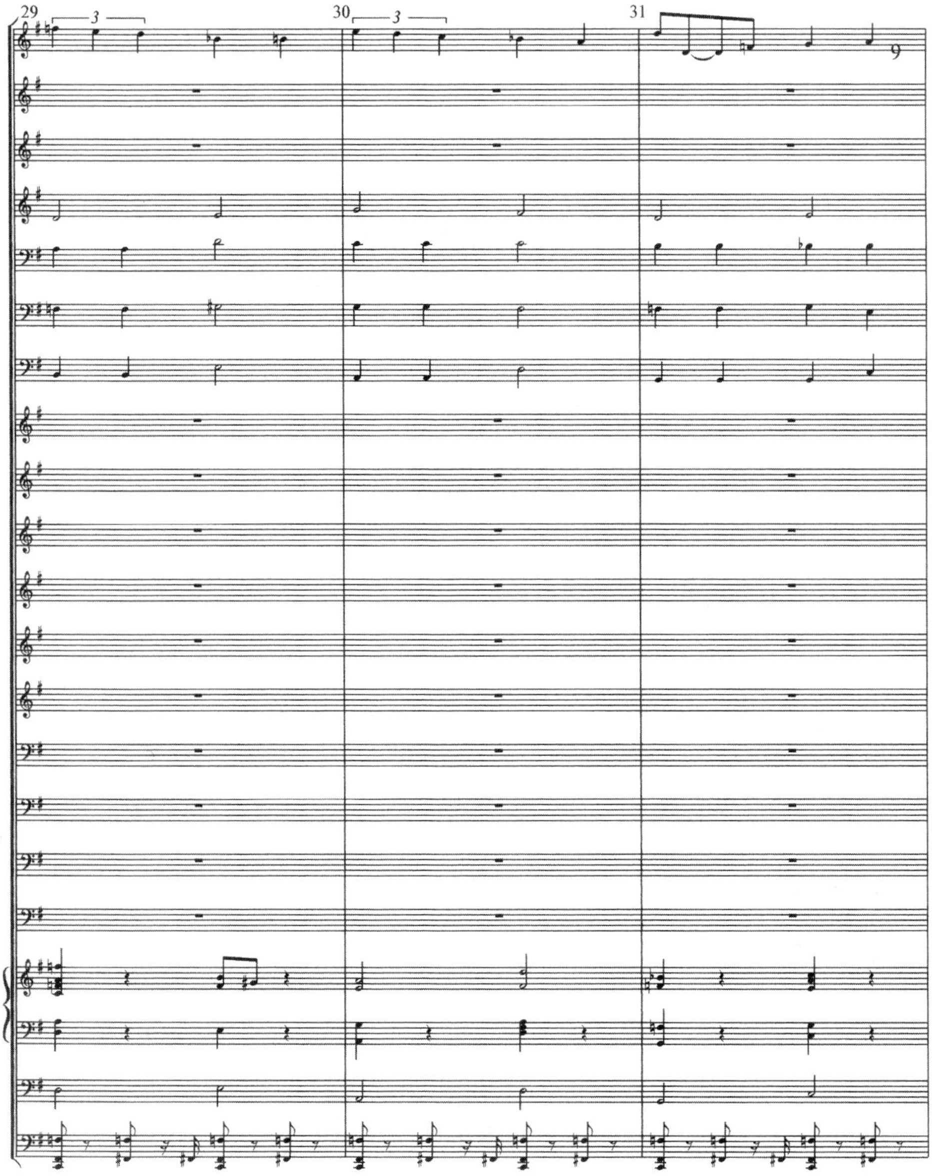
29
3
30
3
31
9

Flying and Feeling So Fine

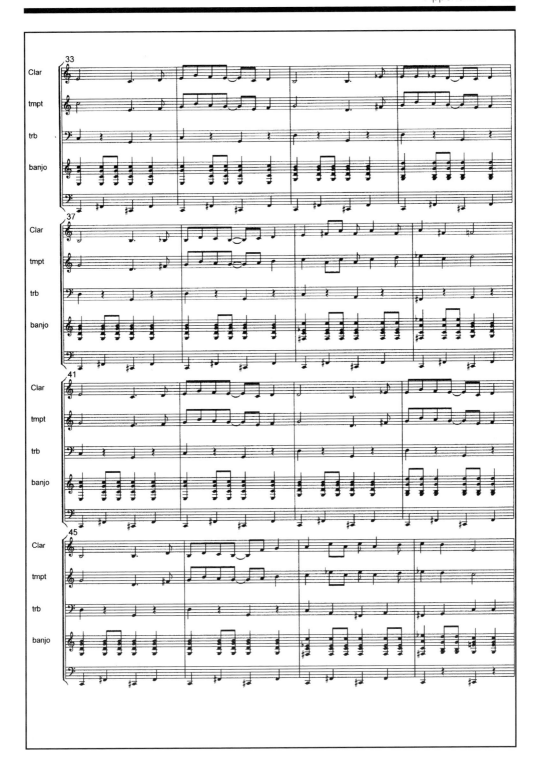

5

Drive Me Crazy

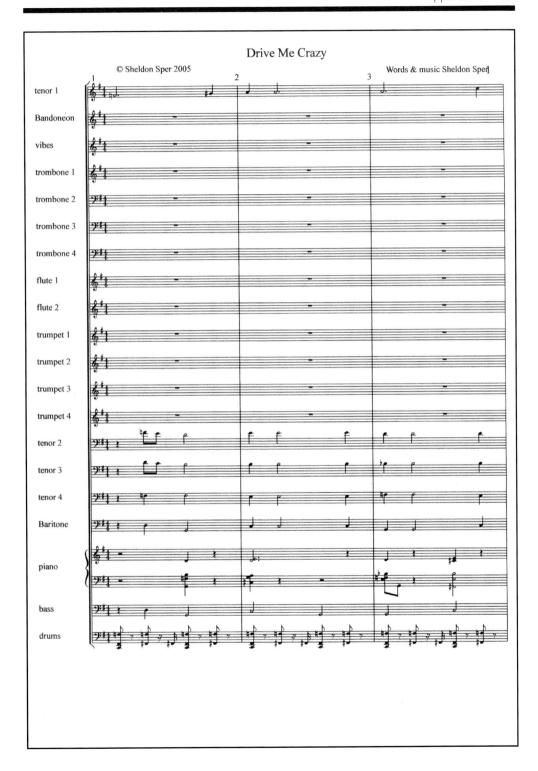

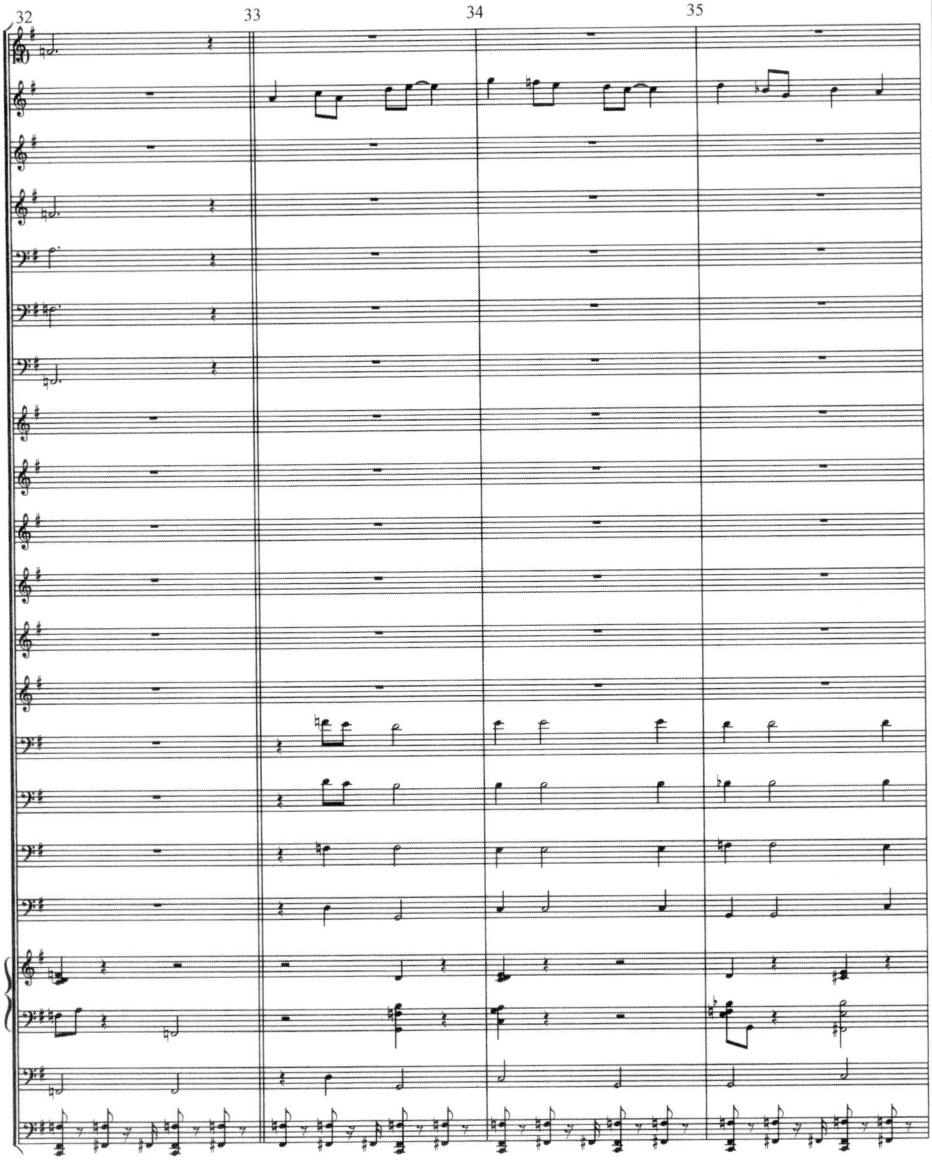
32
33
34
35

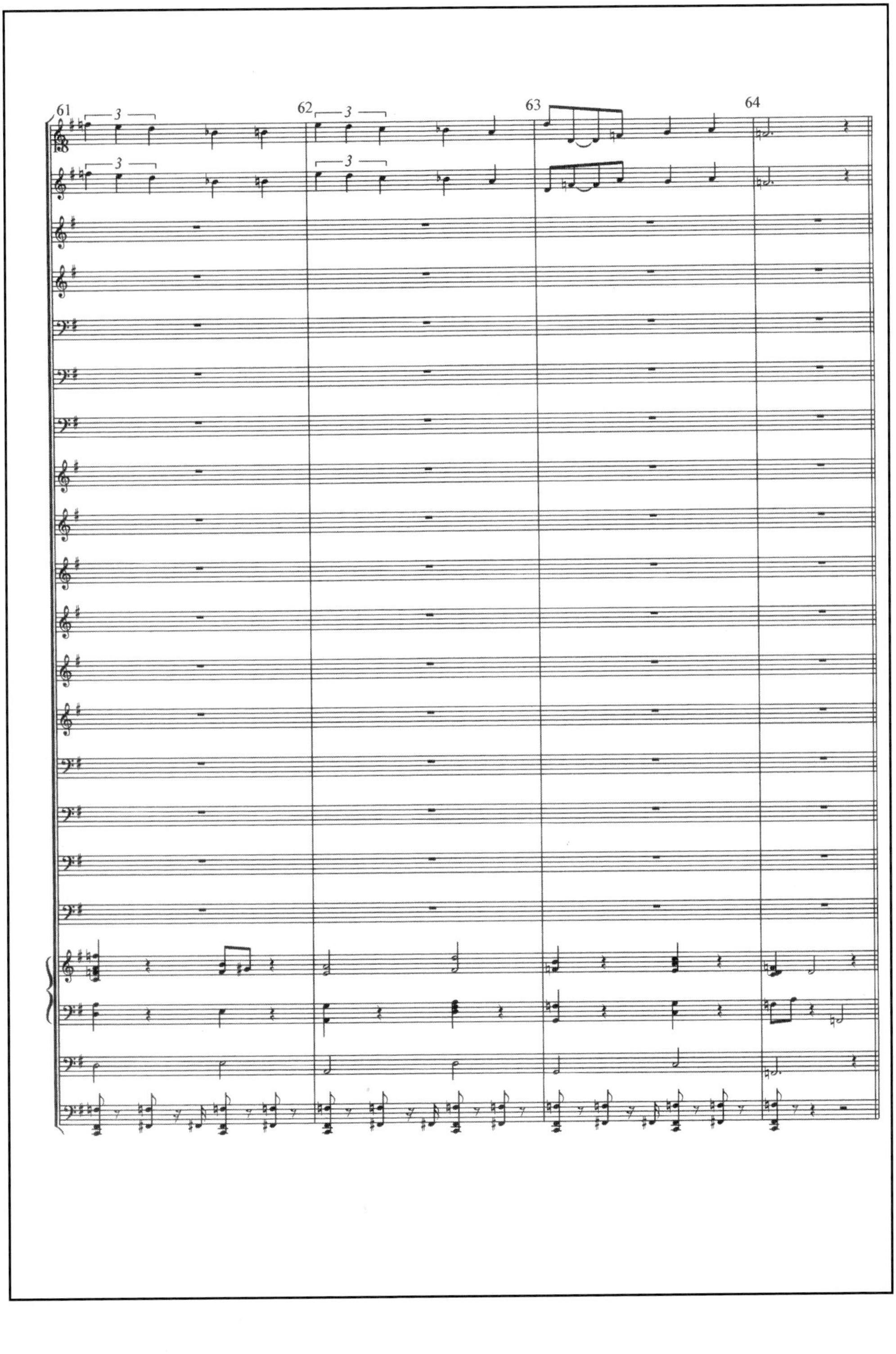
61
62
63
64
3

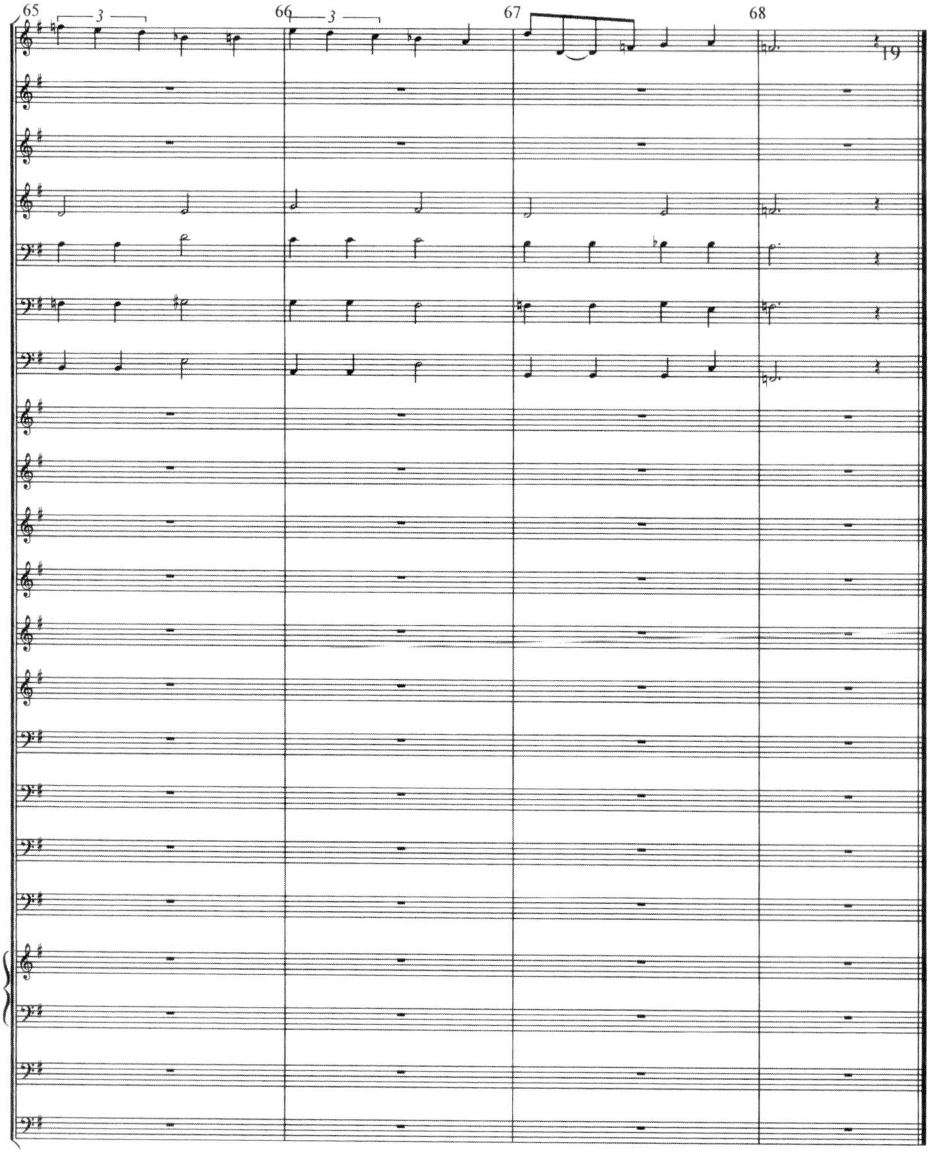
65
3
66
3
67
68
19

This is not a real index.   The book is small, and if you want to look something up, you will be sent to the first mention of that subject.   For example, the Matrix Screen is mentioned thirty or forty times throughout the book, it would be tedious to list its every occurrence.